ARTIFICIAL

INTELLIGENCE 2023

Learn Everything About the Revolution of

Artificial Intelligence.

LIAM HARRISON

TABLE OF CONTENTS

Introduction

We enthusiastically welcome you to the dawn of a new era. In the year 2023, the world finds itself in the midst of profound transformation brought about by an engineering marvel known as artificial intelligence (AI). As we stand poised on the threshold of entering a period that will establish unprecedented norms, it is critically important that we appreciate the breadth of its impacts and capitalize on the opportunities they present.

Owing to the tremendous advancements made in AI technology, it has emerged as one of the most significant developments of the decade.

What began as a concept in science fiction has now become a tangible force reshaping daily life, disrupting entire industries, and pushing the boundaries of what was previously fathomable. Its influence can be seen across diverse domains including healthcare, banking, education, transportation, and entertainment, fundamentally altering the ways we conduct business, interact, and experience the world.

In the course "ARTIFICIAL INTELLIGENCE 2023," we embark on a journey to explore the remarkable phenomenon of artificial intelligence and uncover its transformative potential. This book will serve as your guide, equipping you with an in-depth understanding of AI and the skills to navigate this new landscape with confidence.

This book is for you if you are an entrepreneur interested in leveraging the disruptive power of artificial intelligence, a professional wondering about its impact on your field, or an individual simply fascinated by the possibilities on the horizon. In this course, we will examine the foundational concepts underpinning AI, as well as its myriad applications and ethical considerations surrounding implementation. Additionally, we will explore practical techniques to capitalize on AI's introduction into the marketplace and maximize opportunities for personal and professional growth.

Join us as we delve into the intricacies of natural language processing, robotics, deep neural networks, and machine learning. Discover how artificial intelligence is enhancing customer experiences, streamlining business operations, and changing healthcare service delivery. Get ready to unravel the hidden logic behind AI-driven decision making, automated processes, and predictive analytics. Embrace the prospects in AI-fueled innovation, and prepare to thrive in this rapid-paced, ever-evolving arena.

The time to harness AI is now. Artificial intelligence's presence grows more ubiquitous by the day, increasingly permeating our lives. By unraveling its complexity and grasping its implications, we can tap into its power to propel ourselves into a future defined by creativity, efficiency, and infinite possibilities.

Are you ready to embark on this journey that will profoundly transform you? Let's dive headfirst into the world of AI to uncover its limitless potential together. We are delighted you are joining us here at "ARTIFICIAL INTELLIGENCE 2023."

Chapter One

What is Artificial Intelligence (AI)?

The process of constructing computer systems that are capable of carrying out activities that would ordinarily need the intellect of a human being is referred to as "artificial intelligence" (AI), which is an abbreviation for the word. It comprises the manufacturing of intelligent machines that are able to learn, reason, and figure out solutions to issues as well as come to their own conclusions. The term "artificial intelligence" (AI) refers to an umbrella term that encompasses a number of different subfields, some of which include machine learning, natural language processing, computer vision, robotics, and expert systems.

The significance of artificial intelligence in today's world is something that both can't be understated and absolutely must be acknowledged. It has the potential to transform a broad range of aspects of our lives, including our industries, our healthcare system, our transportation system, our communication system, and even our government. When contemplating the relevance of AI, there are a number of crucial considerations to bear in mind, including the following:

- Increased Productivity and Task Mechanization

Artificial intelligence (AI) technologies make it feasible to automate monotonous and repetitive tasks, freeing up human resources for activities that demand a higher level of complexity and creativity. This leads to greater efficiency, output, and cost-effectiveness across a wide range of diverse sectors of the economy. For instance, in the manufacturing business, AI-powered robots can carry out repetitive assembly line activities with accuracy and speed, leading to increased production and a decrease in the number of mistakes that occur.

AI systems that have had their decision-making skills improved are able to analyze vast amounts of data, identify patterns, and draw helpful insights to assist in the process of decision-making. This may help businesses optimize operations, better forecast trends in the market, and build plans that are more likely to be successful. In the realm of medicine, artificial intelligence algorithms may give support to medical practitioners in the diagnosis of diseases, the suggestion of therapies, and the prediction of patient outcomes based on the analysis of large-scale amounts of patient data.

• Customization, in addition to the Emphasis Placed on the Consumer's Experience

By analyzing the tastes and behaviors of users, artificial intelligence makes it possible to have experiences that are more precisely matched to their needs. Platforms such as Netflix and Amazon employ recommendation systems, which provide users with options for content and products based on their individual preferences for a certain category. Both the overall pleasure of customers and their involvement with the platform are increased as a result of this. Customers may get personalised support, including answers to their queries and issue resolution in real time, via chatbots that are powered by artificial intelligence (AI).

- Recent Developments and Achievements in the Field of Research and Scientific Investigations

The process of scientific discoveries and breakthroughs may potentially be sped up by the use of artificial intelligence. Processing and analyzing vast volumes of research data is within the capabilities of algorithms that learn via machine learning. As a result, these algorithms may reveal patterns and correlations that people would overlook. This enables researchers to make significant ground in their respective fields and adds to the growth of a wide variety of areas of scientific research and study, including the creation of drugs, genetics, and climate modeling, to name just a few.

14

• Enhancements As well as being Applied to Diagnostics, Made to Healthcare

The field of medicine is undergoing a change as a result of the introduction of artificial intelligence (AI), which is allowing for more precise diagnostics, earlier illness diagnosis, and more tailored treatment techniques. AI algorithms contribute to the advancement of medical imaging methods like as MRI and CT scans by aiding in the identification of anomalies and the processing of images for the purpose of providing correct diagnoses. This contribution may be seen in the improvement of diagnostic accuracy. In addition, wearable technology and health applications powered by artificial intelligence gather and analyze patient data, which allows remote monitoring and preventive therapies in the healthcare industry.

- Repercussions for Both Society and Individual Morality

When artificial intelligence becomes more integrated into daily life, important ethical and societal problems are posed. Worries about privacy, biases in AI algorithms, job displacement, and the influence on human decision-making are some of the most critical challenges that need to be overcome. There are many other concerns that need to be solved. It is necessary to guarantee that artificial intelligence (AI) is developed and implemented in a way that is ethical and responsible if we are to enjoy the advantages of AI without putting individual rights in jeopardy or increasing social inequities. If we are to reap the benefits of AI, we must ensure that AI is developed and implemented in an ethical and responsible manner.

• The Prospects for the Future

The applications that AI has right now are only the tip of the iceberg when it comes to all of the potential uses for AI. Research that is now being conducted in disciplines such as explainable artificial intelligence, quantum computing, and brain interfacing has the potential to lead to further technological advancements. These results may pave the way for artificial intelligence systems that are more open to the public, able to think, and even able to interact with people on a more profound level. The potential for improved human-computer cooperation and comprehension would be significantly boosted as a result of this development.

The use of artificial intelligence has significant ramifications in the contemporary day and is positioned to have a significant influence on the foreseeable future. Because of its capacity to automate chores, enhance decision-making, personalize experiences, promote scientific research, improve healthcare, and solve social issues, this technology is considered to be disruptive. However, in order to ensure that artificial intelligence will have a positive influence on society, it is imperative that ethical concerns and the development of AI in a responsible manner get a significant amount of attention.

Exploring the historical context and milestones of AI development

Gaining a better understanding of the historical context and important breakthroughs that contributed to the birth of artificial intelligence (AI) may give very helpful insight into the growth and progression of this field of study. The following is a list of some of the most pivotal moments in the development of AI throughout history:

1. Primitive Concepts and Primary Building Blocks (Throughout the Years of the 1940s and 1950s)

• 1943

It was Warren McCulloch and Walter Pitts that came up with the concept of artificial neural networks for the first time. It is generally agreed that these two individuals were the ones who were responsible for building the framework for computer models that are based on the human brain.

• 1950

The groundbreaking research paper "Computing Machinery and Intelligence" was written by Alan Turing, who also came up with the idea of using a test called the Turing Test to determine whether or not a computer has intelligence.

• 1956

The prospects and goals of machine intelligence were a topic of discussion at the Dartmouth Conference, which is often regarded as the "birthplace" of artificial intelligence (AI) as a field of research.

Symbolic artificial intelligence and logic-based computer systems were both developed throughout the 1950s and 1960s.

In the early days of research into artificial intelligence, the major emphasis was on the construction of symbolic systems that solved issues by manipulating logical symbols. These early systems were able to answer complex problems in a very short amount of time.

2. Between the years 1956 and 1961, John McCarthy invented what is now known as LISP, which stands for "List Processing Language."

The LISP programming language was the first of its kind to be developed with the specific purpose of facilitating artificial intelligence.

• 1958

It is generally agreed that John McCarthy was the first person to make use of the phrase "artificial intelligence."

Herbert Simon and Allen Newell developed the first computer program in 1958 and 1959 that was capable of proving mathematical theorems. The Logic Theorist was the name of this piece of software.

• 1963

James Slagle was the person responsible for developing SAINT, an early example of an expert system that was used to find solutions to problems requiring mathematics.

3. The Phenomenal Growth of Symbolic AI in the 1970s and 1980s and Its Subsequent Collapse

Artificial intelligence research eventually shifted its major emphasis to be on knowledge-based systems, rule-based expert systems, and symbolic reasoning.

• 1973

The MYCIN system developed by Edward Shortliffe has shown diagnostic skills that are on par with those of a seasoned professional in the area of infectious diseases.

• 1980

The early models for 3D object identification that David Marr created were critical to the development of the area of machine vision and helped propel it forward at a rapid pace.

In the late 1980s, Symbolic AI was having difficulty overcoming limitations in its capacity to deal with ambiguity, real-world complexity, and large-scale data sets. This was a contributing factor to the AI winter, which was a period of time during which there was a decrease in funding and interest in AI research.

4. The ideas of connectionism and neural networks gained popularity throughout the 1980s and 1990s.

Researchers' interest in this area of study has recently seen a rebirth because to the capability of neural networks to learn and adapt based on the data they are exposed to.

In 1986, a seminal study on backpropagation, a training technique for multi-layer neural networks, was published. The paper made significant contributions to the field. Geoff

Hinton, David Rumelhart, and Ronald Williams were all contributors to the paper that was written.

- 1987

It was made feasible to do more complex sequence learning tasks by the creation of recurrent neural networks and the design of long-term short-term memory (LSTM).

In 1997, IBM's Deep Blue demonstrated the usefulness of artificial intelligence (AI) in both tactical and strategic decision-making by defeating Garry Kasparov, the reigning world chess champion at the time.

Both machine learning and big data have seen explosive growth since the turn of the century.

The subject of artificial intelligence research has recently seen something of a renaissance because, in large part, to developments in machine learning algorithms, advances in computing power, and the accessibility of vast quantities of data.

Geoffrey Hinton and his colleagues came up with the first concept for deep learning algorithms in the year 2006. These techniques resulted in a significant improvement in the performance of neural networks across a wide range of different applications.

• In 2011, IBM's Watson prevailed on the game program Jeopardy!, demonstrating the capability of AI systems to interpret everyday language and handle enormous quantities of data.

• In the year 2012, a deep convolutional neural network by the name of AlexNet produced a substantial breakthrough in the accuracy of image classification, which cleared the door for big leaps ahead in the area of computer vision.

• In 2014, DeepMind's AlphaGo defeated Lee Sedol, the reigning world champion of the board game Go, proving AI's potential to master tough games that need both intuition and strategic thinking. This demonstrates AI's capacity to master difficult games that require both intuition and strategic thought.

5. The Most Recent Events and the Direction in Which Things Are Moving

In the last several years, there have been substantial advancements made in a variety of domains, including the processing of natural languages, reinforcement learning, generative models, and robotics, to name just a few.

Applications of artificial intelligence are gradually being implemented into day-to-day activities. Some examples of these applications include virtual assistants, driverless cars, recommendation systems, and individualized healthcare.

The ethical and social consequences of artificial intelligence (AI) are receiving an increasing amount of attention, and attempts are being undertaken to address biases, transparency, accountability, and the responsible deployment of AI systems.

It is possible to track the development of artificial intelligence all the way up to the current day, when AI is driving the growth of technical developments. The evolution of artificial intelligence can be followed all the way back to its first concepts and continued all the way up to the present day. Throughout the course of its existence, the industry has been a participant in a number of significant technological breakthroughs, paradigm changes, as well as times of both enthusiasm and skepticism. The continuous advancements

30

in artificial intelligence (AI) and the directions it will go in the future have a huge amount of potential to revolutionize many different aspects of our society and to steer the development of future technologies. This potential can be seen in the massive amount of disruptive power that AI now has.

An examination of the influence that artificial intelligence has had across a variety of sectors and on society as a whole

Significant and far-reaching changes are going to be brought about by artificial intelligence (AI) in a number of fields of the business as well as in society as a whole. A paradigm change is now occurring in artificial intelligence

(AI) technology, which is leading to the disruption of traditional business models, the reinvention of whole sectors, and the altering of how people live, work, and interact with one another. In this part, we will study the impact that AI has had across a range of different businesses, in addition to the larger social consequences of AI and how it has affected society.

1. Healthcare

Medical imaging analysis, which includes X-rays, CT scans, and MRIs, is made easier with the use of AI algorithms. This makes it possible to identify and diagnose illnesses more accurately. Analysis of medical images, which is made possible with the aid of AI algorithms, is an essential step in the treatment of a variety of medical problems. It enables early diagnosis as well as a more accurate diagnosis, which ultimately leads to better results for the patient.

By employing AI to assist in finding potential therapeutic candidates, the process of drug discovery may be sped up, and the costs associated with research and development can be reduced.

Artificial intelligence examines vast quantities of patient data to tailor treatment regimens, predict patient outcomes, and uncover novel solutions based on the characteristics and medical history of an individual patient.

Personalized medicine is the name given to this subspecialty of medicine.

Monitoring from a Distance: Wearable technologies and systems powered by artificial intelligence make it feasible to remotely monitor patients, which enhances the quality of care patients get while they are treated at home and permits early intervention in emergency circumstances.

2. Manufacturing and Automated Industrial Processes

• Robotics and other forms of autonomous system: In the industrial and logistics sectors, increased productivity, accuracy, and worker safety may be achieved via the use of AI-driven robots and autonomous systems to automate potentially hazardous and repetitive tasks. Additionally, AI algorithms can analyse sensor data to predict when equipment will break down. This allows preventative maintenance, which in turn reduces the amount of time spent offline and improves the efficiency of the manufacturing operations. Intelligent maintenance strategies such as predictive maintenance are one example.

• Management of the Supply Chain Artificial intelligence may assist in the management of supply chain operations by helping to estimate demand, optimize inventory levels, and expedite deliveries. This, in turn, can assist in lowering costs and improving productivity.

3. The World of Banking and Financial Transactions

In the process of detecting fraud, computers powered by artificial intelligence comb through enormous amounts of financial data in search of irregularities and repeating trends. Because of this, it is now able to recognize fraudulent activities, which also helps to strengthen security measures.

Systems that are driven by AI provide aid in risk assessment, which may be used for the purposes of insurance underwriting, loan approvals, and investment choices. This helps to enhance both the accuracy and the efficiency of these processes.

Support for Customers as Well as Individualized Recommendations

Chatbots and virtual assistants that are powered by artificial intelligence may provide individualized support to customers, make suggestions about products, and provide guidance on financial planning.

4. Transportation: Self-Driving Cars and Other Unmanned Vehicles The use of artificial intelligence (AI) is a crucial part of the process of developing self-driving automobiles and other kinds of autonomous vehicles. It makes driving less dangerous, reduces the negative effects of traffic congestion, and brings novel solutions to problems with mobility.

• Optimization of Routes: Artificial intelligence systems may enhance transportation routes based on real-time data, which leads to a reduction in emissions and fuel consumption while simultaneously boosting the efficiency of logistics.

• Increased Reliability as well as Enhancements to the Traveler Experience Because of Predictive Maintenance, AI is helping to anticipate and avoid problems in transportation infrastructure, such as airports and trains, which results to an increase in both the reliability of the infrastructure and the passenger experience.

5. Shopping both in stores and on the internet

• Systems for Making Recommendations: By using AI-powered recommendation algorithms, product recommendations can be provided in a manner that is more personalized. This not only enhances the entire customer experience but also helps to raise sales.

• AI analyzes historical data, current trends, and consumer behavior to improve supply chain efficiency by optimizing inventory levels, reducing waste, and eliminating unnecessary steps in the process. Management of Stock and Supplies Inventory management is one of the applications for artificial intelligence (AI). AI allows visual search capabilities, which let consumers search for items using photos. AI has also enabled the development of capabilities for virtual trying on of clothing. The use of artificial intelligence in the form of tools that allow customers to virtually try on merchandise enhances the quality of the experience of shopping online.

6. Instructional Methods That Are Powered by AI And Are Called Adaptive Learning Platforms Make available Personalized Educational Content, and Tailor the Learning Experience to the Specific Requirements and Achievements of Each Student Through the use of adaptive learning systems that are driven by AI, individualized instructional material is made available.

• Intelligent Tutoring Systems: AI systems have the potential to take on the role of virtual tutors, providing students with tailored feedback, replying to their questions, and guiding them along their educational path.

• Administrative tasks: Artificial intelligence has the potential to automate administrative tasks including as grading and data analysis, freeing up instructors' time to engage in more substantive interactions with their students.

7. The Repercussions for Society

• Employment and Workforce: There is a risk that employment could be lost due to automation that is induced by AI in some areas. This might have a negative impact on the

41

workforce. On the other hand, this also leads in the creation of new career prospects, notably in the sphere of artificial intelligence (AI) development and AI-augmented professions that need the application of human abilities.

• Taking Into Account Ethical Concerns Ethical problems are raised by artificial intelligence, including the possibility of prejudice in computer programs, breaches of personal privacy, possible risks to data security, and the need that AI be used in decision-making processes in a responsible manner.

• Accessibility and Inclusion: Artificial intelligence has the potential to overcome accessibility difficulties, making it simpler for people with disabilities to navigate the physical environment and access information. This might be a significant step toward achieving the goal of full inclusion.

• Impact on the Economy: The innovations that are the result of artificial intelligence have the potential to contribute to economic development, advances in productivity, and the establishment of new industries and markets.

The influence that artificial intelligence has on a wide range of businesses and on society as a whole may be described as revolutionary. Across a broad spectrum of businesses, including as healthcare, manufacturing, banking, transportation, retail, and education, there is an increase in productivity, accuracy, and the capacity to make intelligent choices as a result of the use of AI. It does provide a great many advantages, but it also introduces a great many challenges that need careful attention to be paid to them. Ethical issues, job loss, and ensuring that access and participation are provided on an equitable basis for all parties involved are just some of the problems that need to be solved. It is crucial to establish a balance between the possibilities given by AI and the development of the technology in a responsible and ethical way in order to completely harness the potential of artificial intelligence for the benefit of society. This is necessary in order to fully harness the potential

of AI for the good of society.

Chapter Two

AI Basics

The study and use of artificial intelligence (AI) is a varied area of research and practice that comprises the construction and deployment of computer systems that are capable of executing activities that would normally need the intellect of people. This field of study and practice has been more popular in recent years. The essential principles and concepts that drive artificial intelligence revolve on modeling and replicating human intellect with the use of computer algorithms, data, and processing capability. This may be accomplished by modeling human intelligence using computer data. During the course of this discussion, we are going to go even further into these concepts and explore them in more detail.

• Learning by Machines (often abbreviated as ML)

Machine learning is a central concept in the study of artificial intelligence (AI), which focuses on the creation of algorithms and models that are able to learn from data without being specifically programmed to do so. AI is a subfield of the subject of computer science. It entails educating a computer system to recognize patterns, make predictions, or make judgements based on the knowledge it has gathered through being exposed to a significant dataset. Machine learning may be approached in many different ways, the most common of which are supervised learning, unsupervised learning, and reinforcement learning. All of these categories are quite all-encompassing.

• Neural Networks Created Artificially

Neural networks are a kind of algorithm that are called after the manner in which the human brain is structured and the ways in which it executes its many functions. Neurons, which are nodes in a network of linked nodes, are stacked in layers and provide the basis of these structures. Every neuron in the network takes in information, applies some kind of activation function to that information, and then passes on the outcome to the neuron on the layer below it. Image and audio recognition, natural language processing, and generative modeling are just a few of the fields that benefit substantially from the capabilities of neural networks, which include the capacity to recognize complex patterns and correlations in data. Neural networks also have the ability to handle large amounts of data very quickly.

• Learning at a Deep Level

Deep learning is a branch of machine learning that includes the training of hierarchical data representations by using "deep" neural networks that contain several layers. This area of machine learning is referred to as "deep learning." It bestows to the model the capability of automatically extracting high-level characteristics from raw input, which, in the end, results in improved performance in tasks like as computer vision and natural language processing. Deep learning is credited with helping to usher in a new age of artificial intelligence (AI) by obtaining state-of-the-art results in a range of sectors and setting the way for improvements in industries such as autonomous cars and medical diagnostics. This was accomplished by producing state-of-the-art outcomes in a variety of fields.

- The processing of natural language, commonly known as natural language processing (NLP)

Natural language processing, sometimes known as NLP, is an area of artificial intelligence that investigates how humans and computers can interact with one another through language. To be more specific, it refers to the process of building models and algorithms that are able to grasp, analyze, and synthesize meaningful human language. Natural language processing (NLP) is a technique that makes it possible to do a variety of language-related tasks, such as sentiment analysis, machine translation, text summarization, chatbots, and voice assistants.

This area encompasses a wide range of methodologies, including tokenization, part-of-speech tagging, named entity recognition, and sentiment analysis, to mention a few.

• Vision Through the Use of Computers

The purpose of the field of computer vision is to provide computers the capacity to develop a visual understanding by analyzing digital still images or moving pictures. To be more specific, it comprises the development of algorithms and models that are in a position to interpret and assess visual data in a manner that is comparable to the way in which people experience the environment. Picture classification, object identification and tracking, face recognition, image captioning, and autonomous driving are all examples of applications for computer vision technology. Image captioning is another use of this technology. The use of convolutional neural networks, more often referred to by its abbreviation CNN, is common in computer vision applications.

• Instruction Based on Positive and Negative Feedback

Reinforcement learning is a subfield of machine learning that focuses on training computers to make sequential judgements by having the computers participate in dialogue with their environment. This is done to educate the computers how to learn. The agent is able to acquire new knowledge as a result of the feedback it gets, which, depending on the actions it takes, may take the shape of rewards or sanctions. Positive outcomes have been achieved by applying reinforcement learning to a variety of endeavors, including game playing, robotics, resource management, and recommendation systems. Reinforcement learning employs a variety of techniques, including Q-learning, policy gradients, and deep reinforcement learning, to name just a few of the more known examples.

• Information and "Big Data"

The fuel that artificial intelligence systems use to power themselves is data. It has become clear that having access to vast volumes of data is one of the most important factors in the process of successfully training AI models. Big data is a word that is used to describe datasets that are both too extensive and too sophisticated to be analyzed using traditional techniques. These datasets are referred to as "Big Data." Big data technology is used by artificial intelligence (AI) to handle, store, and analyze huge volumes of structured and unstructured data. This data may be arranged in a variety of ways. Because it is driven by data, this technique makes it feasible for AI models to learn over time and become more accurate as they do so.

• Artificial intelligence that is both responsible and ethical

As applications of artificial intelligence continue to proliferate across a variety of societal domains, it is imperative that we give serious thought to the ethical implications of these developments. In order to build ethical and responsible AI, it is necessary to design and deploy AI systems that take into consideration concerns pertaining to justice, transparency, privacy, responsibility, and the potential societal effect of the creation of AI application software. It is necessary to make certain that artificial intelligence is deployed ethically and in line with human values in order to avoid biases, discrimination, and other unintended repercussions.

The study of artificial intelligence (AI) is guided by a number of basic principles and concepts, some of which are listed below. However, it is crucial to bear in mind that AI is a science that is experiencing fast growth, and that the ongoing research and development in this field continuously modifies and expands our understanding of these ideas. This is something that should be kept in mind at all times.

Deep learning, neural networks, and machine learning are all topics that will be discussed.

1. The concept of machine learning:

Machine learning is an area of artificial intelligence that focuses on the design of algorithms and models that can learn from data and make predictions or decisions without being explicitly programmed to do so. This is accomplished via the use of deep learning techniques. It is premised on the idea that computers are able to learn patterns and correlations from large datasets, and then generalize that knowledge in order to make predictions on new data that has never been seen before. This theory underpins the notion of machine learning.

Learning that takes place inside of a computer may be divided up into three basic groups: supervised learning, unsupervised learning, and reinforcement learning.

• Education and Training Via Supervision

During the training phase of supervised learning, the model is educated with the use of data that has been annotated. This indicates that the data being entered are coupled with the value that matches to the goal being sought. The job of the model is to figure out how to translate the variables that are being input into the system to the variables that are being produced from the system. The categorization of images, the recognition of speech, and the detection of spam are all instances of activities that are examples of tasks that come within the area of supervised learning.

- Learning on One's Own Without Direct Instruction

Unsupervised learning is a kind of machine learning that involves the examination of data that has not been labeled. This type of learning requires the model to uncover patterns, structures, or connections within the data on its own, without being given any particular instructions. Clustering and dimensionality reduction are two methods that see a lot of application in the field of unsupervised learning. Both clustering algorithms and dimensionality reduction strategies aim to represent high-dimensional data in a lower-dimensional space while preserving the integrity of vital information. This is accomplished via the use of reduced dimensions. On the other hand, dimensionality reduction approaches perform the reverse of what clustering algorithms do, which is to group together data points that are similar to one another.

• Instruction Based on Positive and Negative Feedback

As part of the process of reinforcement learning, an agent learns how to make a sequence of choices by interacting with an environment. This learning takes place over time. The agent receives feedback in the form of incentives or penalties in line with the acts that it has performed, and the feedback is based on the actions that it has taken. The agent learns how to maximize its rewards via a process of trial and error, which involves discovering the most effective behaviors to do in a range of circumstances in order to achieve the best possible outcomes. Reinforcement learning has been effectively employed in a variety of areas, including game playing, robotics, and the management of resources, to name just a few of those fields.

2. Neural Networks, Also Known As

Neural networks are a category of computational models that derive their inspiration from the structure and function of the human brain. Artificial neurons, which are also referred to as connected nodes, are used to construct them, and they are organized in layers. Every neuron in the network receives signals as input, applies an activation function to those signals, and then generates an output signal that is sent to the layer below it. These signals are then processed by the neuron that receives them.

The following is a list of the major components that contribute to the formation of a neural network:

• The First Layer of Input

At this point in the process, the input layer is responsible for bringing in any initial data or characteristics that need to be processed.

• Secret Concealed Levels

Both the input layer and the output layer have a number of additional layers known as intermediate layers concealed in between them. During the process, a variety of weighted connections and activation functions are used. During this time, these components carry out computations and change the data that is being received.

• The Layer That Handles Output

The layer of the neural network that is selected to be the output is the node that is responsible for producing the network's ultimate output or prediction.

In neural networks, learning happens when the weights that are assigned to the connections between neurons are updated depending on the data that is used for training. This data is used to teach the network new information. Backpropagation is the name given to the technique that is used in the process of making this modification. Backpropagation is the process of propagating errors that arise between the expected output and the actual target values back through the network and adjusting the weights appropriately.

Backpropagation is also known as error propagation. The learning process will continue to cycle through its many iterations until the model achieves the required degree of precision in its predictions.

3. Deep Learning: Deep learning is a branch of machine learning that focuses on neural networks that have several hidden layers. 4. Reinforcement Learning: Reinforcement learning is a technique that utilizes feedback to improve performance. These networks were developed with the purpose of learning difficult knowledge. Deep neural networks are able to generate hierarchical representations of data, which enables them to automatically extract higher-level properties from raw input.

This ability allows deep neural networks to outperform traditional machine learning techniques. • Due to the vastness of the network, it is feasible to develop intricate models that are able to handle a large number of different data sets. This is a huge benefit when compared to standard machine learning approaches. Deep learning has received a lot of interest and generated outstanding results in a variety of different domains, including computer vision, natural language processing, and voice recognition, amongst others. This is due to the fact that deep learning can more accurately model complex data sets than conventional machine learning techniques.

• CNNs, which is an abbreviation that stands for "convolutional neural networks," are a kind of "deep neural network" that are used often in activities that are associated with computer vision. They are taught to detect visual patterns by using convolutional layers in order to extract local properties from the pictures they are provided with. This allows the computers to be trained to recognize visual patterns. CNNs have attained a level of performance that is regarded to be state-of-the-art in many fields, including image classification, object identification, and picture segmentation.

•RNNs, which stands for "recurrent neural networks," are a kind of deep neural network that are classified as a subclass. These networks have the capability of processing sequential data, such as time series or sequences derived from natural language. RNNs feature a memory component that allows them to record temporal connections and context, which enables them to be helpful for tasks such as machine translation, voice recognition, and sentiment analysis. RNNs also contain a memory component that enables them to record temporal relationships and context. RNNs are also capable of acquiring new knowledge and becoming better over time.

One of the most important advantages of using deep learning is that it does away with the need for human feature engineering. This is one of the most major benefits of using the approach.

The process of deep learning allows for the automated learning of hierarchical representations. Models trained using deep learning can handle enormous datasets, identify complex patterns, and carry out their tasks with a high degree of precision. Deep learning models, on the other hand, often need a large amount of computing resources in addition to a big number of labeled data in order to be adequately trained. This is because deep learning models are more complicated.

Learning algorithms that are implemented in modern AI systems include machine learning, learning using neural networks, and deep learning. Neural networks, and especially deep neural networks, allow the development of sophisticated models that can learn hierarchical representations and achieve exceptional performance in a range of AI tasks. Machine learning offers the foundation for training models on data. This capacity is made possible, in particular, by deep neural networks.

Introducing key algorithms and techniques used in AI systems

AI systems make use of a large array of algorithmic and methodological techniques in order to allow a range of features and manage difficult difficulties. These approaches may be categorized as either formal or informal. During the course of this discussion, we are going to look at a wide variety of essential algorithms and procedures that are often implemented in AI systems.

• The implementation of Trees of Decision

Decision trees are hierarchical models that generate judgements or predictions by recursively dividing the input space depending on certain features. These judgments or predictions may be used in a variety of contexts. The data may be used to generate these conclusions or make these forecasts. They play a significant role in a wide range of classification and regression procedures and are used widely in both. Some examples of decision tree algorithms are ID3, C4.5, and CART. These algorithms construct trees by selecting the optimal split criteria at each node, which, in the end, results in a series of binary choices that lead to the final forecast.

• Forests Chosen at Random

Random forests are a form of ensemble learning approach that incorporate a number of distinct decision trees in order to improve both the accuracy and resilience of the learning process. They do this by using a subset of features and bootstrap sampling of the training data for each tree, which ultimately leads to the implementation of randomization in the system. Random forests may be put to use for a wide number of tasks, such as classification, regression, and the evaluation of the relative relevance of various features. They have the capability of processing data with a high dimension.

• Support vector machines, also known as SVMs.

The Support Vector Machine (SVM) is an advanced technology that may be used for classification and regression work respectively. The most important aspect of its functioning is locating an ideal hyperplane that properly anticipates continuous value ranges or maximizes the number of data points that may be separated into different groups. SVMs are able to deal with high-dimensional data, perform magnificently with small to medium-sized datasets, and employ kernel functions to deal with nonlinear connections in a manner that is both effective and efficient. SVMs also have the capability to deal with high-dimensional data.

• k-Nearest Neighbors, sometimes known as k-NN because of its abbreviation

The k-NN algorithm is a non-parametric methodology that may be applied for classification and regression analysis. This method was developed by Google. It does this by scanning the feature space for the k closest neighbors, after which it either assigns the class that has the majority of votes or it averages the values of those neighbors. Because of this, it is able to make predictions. Although it is simple to understand, the performance of the k-NN method is very sensitive to the distance metric used as well as the value that is selected for the k parameter.

• The Ignorant Bayes

The Bayes' theorem is the cornerstone of the probabilistic algorithm that is often referred to as the Naive Bayes algorithm. The term "naive" comes from the assumption that separate features do not interact with one another, which is the basis of this theory. Because they are effective, scalable, and rapid, Naive Bayes models are useful for text classification, spam filtering, and recommendation systems. Even though it is assumed that they are autonomous, they regularly attain competitive levels of performance.

• Principal Component Analysis, or PCA for short.

PCA is a technique that compresses high-dimensional data into a lower-dimensional space while preserving the integrity of the data's fundamental components. This allows for a reduction in the number of dimensions that the data occupies. The identification of orthogonal axes, sometimes referred to as major components, that are responsible for the highest amount of variation in the data is the method that is used to achieve this goal. PCA is put to considerable use in a wide range of applications, such as data compression, noise reduction, and visualization.

• Methods of organizing data into groups using algorithms

The inherent characteristics of the data points themselves or their spatial closeness to one another in the feature space may be used as a foundation for clustering algorithms, which group together data points that have similarities. A few examples of common clustering algorithms are the k-means method, hierarchical clustering, and the DBSCAN algorithm. The identification of abnormalities and the segmentation of both photos and customers are just two examples of the many applications that clustering may have in modern business.

• RNNs, more often known as "recurrent neural networks."

Recurrent neural networks (RNNs) are a subclass of the neural network category known as recurrent neural networks (RNNs). By adding feedback links in their design, these networks were given the ability to interpret sequential input. Because of the memory capabilities they possess, they are able to recognize temporal dynamics and dependencies in the surrounding environment. Natural language processing, voice recognition, and the analysis of time series data are just some of the applications that make extensive use of RNNs.

"CNN" is an abbreviation for "convolutional neural networks."

CNNs are a kind of neural network that was designed specifically for the purpose of processing grid-like data, such as that which is observed in movies and photographs. They make use of convolutional layers in order to extract local attributes and hierarchical representations from the data that is input into the system. This is accomplished by using the data to train a neural network. The development of CNNs has led to revolutionary changes in a variety of computer vision applications, including the categorization of images, the identification of objects, and the generation of images.

• GAN, sometimes referred to as "generative adversarial networks."

A GAN is a kind of deep learning model that is comprised of a generator network and a discriminator network. GANs are a category of models that fall under the umbrella of deep learning. During the time that the discriminator network is learning to distinguish between real and manufactured data, the generator network is being instructed on how to generate data instances that are accurate representations of the actual world. GANs have shown a high degree of effectiveness when it comes to the development of realistic pictures, text, and audio. Other types of learning algorithms, such as reinforcement learning, have not been as successful.

When reinforcement learning algorithms are put into practice, it is possible for agents to learn how to interact most effectively with their environments via a process of trial and error. Q-learning, policy gradients, and actor-critic techniques are a few examples of the types of algorithms that fall within this category. Reinforcement learning has been effectively used in a variety of domains, including game playing, robotics, and autonomous systems, to name just a few of these applications.

• Approaches that make use of Natural Language Processing (NLP) techniques

It is feasible for computers to read, interpret, and synthesize human language thanks to a variety of natural language processing (NLP) methods, such as tokenization, part-of-speech tagging, named entity identification, and sentiment analysis. These approaches were developed by researchers. NLP algorithms employ machine learning and deep learning strategies in order to analyze text input and generate information with meaning. This is accomplished by combining the two types of learning.

These are only a few instances of the algorithms and procedures that are applied in systems that are powered by artificial intelligence. The area of artificial intelligence (AI) is fairly wide and is continually growing, with new algorithms and techniques being devised and refined on a regular basis in order to solve issues that are getting more complex and to expand the capabilities of AI systems. This is done in order to handle problems that are becoming increasingly complex and to enhance the capabilities of AI systems.

Chapter Three

The Adoption AI

The widespread use of artificial intelligence (AI) across a range of business sectors has not only had a substantial effect on the operations of companies but also on the ways in which people interact with technology in their day-to-day lives. This is because AI has the ability to learn and improve itself over time. The process of programming computer systems to perform out tasks that would typically need the intellect of a human person to carry out, such as visual perception, voice recognition, decision-making, and problem-solving, is referred to as "artificial intelligence" (AI), which is an abbreviation for the word artificial intelligence. Let's begin our inquiry into the widespread use of artificial intelligence across a wide range of industries, as well as the implications of this phenomena.

• Healthcare

The field of medicine has been profoundly altered by the use of artificial intelligence. It has the potential of analyzing huge volumes of patient data, which may assist in the diagnosis of illnesses, the prediction of outcomes, and the recommendation of tailored treatment regimens. Machine learning algorithms may be used to search through medical records, imaging data, and genetic information, all of which allow for the detection of trends and the giving of helpful insights. In addition, chatbots and other forms of AI-powered virtual assistants are being used to improve patient interaction and offer patients with fundamental medical guidance.

• Finance

The use of artificial intelligence in the financial sector has led to the automation of operations, the reduction of expenditures, and an improvement in productivity. Better risk assessment, the detection of fraudulent activities, and algorithmic trading are all possible thanks to the capacity of machine learning algorithms to examine vast amounts of financial data in real time. Chatbots that are powered by AI are finding a growing number of applications, including a range of customer service and support roles, the provision of personalised ideas, and the optimization of financial process.

• Shopping both in stores and on the internet

The use of artificial intelligence (AI) has had a significant and widespread influence on the retail industry, notably on online purchasing. In order to provide customers with tailored product suggestions, recommendation systems that are driven by algorithms powered by artificial intelligence do a study of a customer's behavior, preferences, and purchasing history. This results in an enhanced experience for the client, which in turn boosts sales. Additionally, AI is being applied for the management of inventory, the forecasting of demand, and the optimization of supply chains, all of which result in higher productivity and cost savings as a direct consequence of its application.

• Management of both the Production and Supply Chains

Technologies that use artificial intelligence, such as robots and automation, have fundamentally disrupted the traditional structure of the manufacturing sector. Robots that have been programmed with artificial intelligence are capable of completing difficult jobs quickly while maintaining a high level of accuracy. This results in an increase in industrial output while simultaneously reducing the number of errors made. The optimization of supply chain logistics, route planning, and demand forecasting may be accomplished with the assistance of algorithms that are driven by artificial intelligence. This can result in simplified operations and cost savings.

• Transportation The development of the transportation business is being significantly aided by artificial intelligence, which is playing an important role in this process. The continuous study, development, and testing of autonomous cars controlled by artificial intelligence algorithms has the objective of improving road safety while also reducing the amount of time spent in traffic jams. In order to enhance route planning and provide more accurate arrival time estimates, artificial intelligence is able to analyze real-time traffic data, as well as current weather conditions and historical trends. Additionally, AI is being used to the area of predictive maintenance of autos, with the objectives of optimizing performance while concurrently decreasing downtime. These aims are being pursued via the use of AI.

• Education The capacity of artificial intelligence to provide personalised learning experiences and intelligent tutoring systems has the potential to bring about a paradigm shift in the educational system. Adaptive learning systems, which are driven by algorithms that are powered by artificial intelligence, have the potential to tailor educational material to match the needs, speed, and preferences of individual students. Chatbots driven by artificial intelligence have the ability to make snap judgments, react to questions presented by students, and help with administrative tasks. In addition to this, AI is able to analyze enormous educational datasets, identify trends within those databases, and then apply the findings it makes to enhance educational strategies and policies.

• Matters Relating to the Natural Environment

The energy business is beginning to use AI technology in order to boost productivity, reduce waste, and become a more ecologically responsible enterprise overall. The ability of smart grids to analyze trends of energy consumption, estimate demand, and enhance the efficiency of energy distribution is made possible by the use of artificial intelligence (AI) algorithms. The use of artificial intelligence in the monitoring and management of environmental factors, such as air quality, water supply, and climate change, is another potential use of AI. Because of this, decisions can be made and resources may be distributed with more accuracy.

The broad use of AI raises a number of essential issues and concerns, in addition to raising a number of important potential for progress and advancement. It is necessary to address the ethical problems that surround privacy, security, and bias in order to guarantee the responsible use of artificial intelligence (AI). Additionally, the potential effect that AI might have on the workforce and job displacement should be carefully managed via the use of programs that concentrate on retraining and boosting skill levels. This is because AI could potentially cause job displacement.

The widespread use of AI across a wide range of business sectors is driving significant changes inside those companies, including improvements in the speed and accuracy of decision-making processes, as well as overall company transformation. AI is driving a shift in the way that organizations work and how people interact with technology across a broad variety of industries, from healthcare and finance to retail and transportation. This transition is occurring in all of these different sectors. However, in order to make the most of the potential beneficial benefits of AI, it is necessary to implement it in a cautious way, taking into consideration the consequences that it will have not just for society but also for ethics.

showcasing successful case studies and applications of artificial intelligence in a variety of areas including healthcare, finance, transportation, and more

In the paragraphs that follow, we will go further into some successful case studies and applications of AI in a variety of sectors, including the following:

• Healthcare

a) The Identification of Cancer

When it comes to the processing of medical images for the purpose of identifying cancer, artificial intelligence has shown outstanding performance. For example, the artificial intelligence (AI) system that Google

DeepMind developed was superior than human radiologists in terms of its capacity to identify breast cancer based on mammograms.

b) The Uncovering of New Pharmaceuticals

By sifting through enormous amounts of data in search of potential medicinal compounds, the use of artificial intelligence is helping to hasten the process of drug development. Using AI algorithms, for instance, BenevolentAI was able to uncover a novel therapy option for amyotrophic lateral sclerosis (ALS) in a period of time that was much less than what was needed by traditional approaches. This was accomplished in a lot shorter amount of time.

• Finance

a) The Process of Identifying Fraud

The ability of AI-based algorithms to identify patterns and anomalies in financial transactions, which allows the identification of fraudulent conduct at an earlier stage, is a significant advancement brought about by artificial intelligence. PayPal makes use of artificial intelligence in order to conduct real-time analysis of transactional data. This is done with the intention of preventing fraudulent transactions and safeguarding users.

b) Robotic Advisory System Betterment and Wealthfront are two instances of AI-powered robo-advisory platforms that give customised investment advice and portfolio management based on an individual's objectives, risk tolerance, and the current status of the market. These two platforms are known as Betterment and Wealthfront, respectively.

• Methods of Transportation a) Automobiles Capable of Driving Themselves

Companies like Tesla and Waymo are at the vanguard of the race to build autonomous cars, which depend on artificial intelligence for vision, decision-making, and navigation in order to function safely and effectively. These autos have the potential to make roads safer, reduce the amount of accidents that occur, and increase the efficiency with which transportation may be accomplished.

b) The Administration of Traffic Control

AI-enabled algorithms are able to analyse data on real-time traffic obtained from a range of sources, such as GPS and sensors, in order to enhance the flow of traffic and cut down on congestion. This data may be gathered from a variety of sources. The Smart Nation plan that is being implemented in Singapore uses artificial intelligence to manage the traffic lights and analyze the real-time conditions of the traffic.

• Business in traditional settings as well as on the internet

a) Suggestions that are customized to your particular preferences

E-commerce behemoths such as Amazon and Netflix utilize artificial intelligence algorithms to provide users with individualized product and content suggestions based on the users' tastes, browsing history, and purchase behavior. These recommendations are tailored to the individual user.

b) Artificial intelligence capable of conversation and other types of virtual aid

Chatbots that are powered by artificial intelligence, such as the ones that are used by Sephora and H&M, are able to give individualized assistance to consumers, answer to queries, and provide product suggestions; all of these things lead to an increase in the level of consumer engagement and satisfaction.

• Manufacturing

a) Maintenance Based on Existing Conditions Predictive artificial intelligence algorithms analyze sensor data taken from equipment in order to determine when it will be necessary to perform maintenance and to spot any irregularities. Because of this, preventive maintenance may be performed, and the length of time that equipment must be offline can be cut down. The application of artificial intelligence (AI) in the jet engines produced by General Electric (GE) allows for predictive maintenance to be performed, which in turn reduces the costs associated with maintenance and improves aircraft dependability.

c) Keeping Tabs on the Product's Quality

Both throughout the manufacturing process and after the product has been created, computer vision systems that are fueled by artificial intelligence are able to identify defects and anomalies. For example, Siemens utilizes AI to monitor the manufacture of wind turbine blades in order to discover any problems and maintain consistently high-quality standards. This helps Siemens keep their quality standards continuously high.

Agriculture • Maintaining Vigilance While Monitoring the Crops

Monitoring of crop health, the diagnosis of nutritional deficiencies, and the identification of pests and illnesses are all made possible by the use of artificial intelligence algorithms in combination with satellite imaging. Farmers are able to enhance their total agricultural productivity, optimize the allocation of resources, and decrease crop losses as a direct result of this.

b) Farming with Greater Accuracy Agriculture tasks like planting, spraying, and harvesting might potentially be carried out with millimeter-perfect precision by drones and robots guided by artificial intelligence. This would result in a decrease in the amount of resources that are lost while simultaneously increasing overall production. The Hands Free Hectare project in the UK was able to efficiently accomplish totally autonomous crop production by using both artificial intelligence and robotics. This was made possible by the Hands Free Hectare initiative.

These case studies give examples of the effect that AI has had on many fields and demonstrate the wide and important usage of AI in a range of businesses. The improvement of healthcare outcomes and financial services, the revamping of transportation, and the enhancement of agricultural practices are just some of the areas that are being impacted by the proliferation of artificial intelligence, which is also stimulating innovation in a number of different ways. Even more potential is in store for the not-too-distant future thanks to the continued advancement of artificial intelligence technology and the integration of that technology with other cutting-edge breakthroughs.

Discussing the benefits and challenges associated with implementing AI in business processes

There are many benefits to integrating AI into business processes, but there are also a number of challenges that must be solved. Let's examine the advantages of integrating AI into corporate operations as well as the issues that may arise:

• Benefits of Using AI in Business

1. More efficient use of resources

Artificial intelligence has the power to automate repetitive and time-consuming tasks, enabling businesses to more efficiently deploy resources and run their operations. In the end, this leads to both higher productivity and decreased costs.

Massive amounts of data may be processed swiftly by artificial intelligence with improved decision-making skills, which can then provide insightful information. By providing accurate and current information, artificial intelligence helps organizations to make choices based on data, identify trends, and seize opportunities.

2. Improvement in Customer Experience Quality

Customers may get personalised and prompt support via chatbots and other AI-powered virtual assistants, which raises the overall level of service. Artificial intelligence (AI) algorithms may assess the data that consumers submit and then offer products based on the particular needs of the customer.

3. Advanced Techniques for Data Analysis

AI systems are capable of revealing previously undetected patterns and connections in data that humans would have overlooked. This enables businesses to get deeper understanding of the way their clients behave, market trends, and operational efficiency, which eventually results in better strategic planning and a competitive edge.

4. Risk Reduction

AI has applications in risk management and assessment. For instance, AI systems in the banking industry may look at historical data and current market circumstances to estimate the probability of possible threats and guard against fraudulent practices.

5. Innovation and the Creation of New Possibilities

Artificial intelligence opens up new opportunities for innovation and the development of novel goods and services.

Businesses may use AI to create game-changing solutions, unearth undiscovered markets, and outperform their competitors.

• The Barriers to the Implementation of AI

1. Personality and data integrity protection

The high caliber and precise labeling of the data are crucial for the development of AI models. One of the most challenging components of maintaining data when dealing with sensitive content is assuring its accuracy, completeness, and privacy. Keeping the data's integrity and adhering to privacy laws are two significant barriers to the implementation of AI.

2. Moral and ethical considerations

AI raises questions about morality and ethics, such as algorithmic bias, responsibility, and transparency. In order to ensure fairness and inclusiveness in artificial intelligence systems, biases in data and algorithms must be eliminated since these biases might lead to outputs that are unfair or discriminatory.

Talent and Skills Gap

The use of AI necessitates the training of specialists in data science, machine learning, and other branches of AI technology. Because there is a scarcity of knowledge in these fields, it is challenging for businesses to find and recruit skilled AI personnel.

3. Adding New Components to Current Systems

Successfully integrating AI into an organization's current business activities may be challenging. There is a chance that legacy systems won't operate with AI technology, which would call for significant changes to the infrastructure and procedures. Making ensuring that the integration and interoperability go off without a hitch will be the most crucial responsibility.

4. Regulations as well as Law-Related Concerns

The legal and regulatory environment related to AI is now going through major development. The legal frameworks governing data protection, intellectual property, liability, and responsibility must be well understood by organizations. The need of adhering to several standards and conventions makes the use of AI more challenging.

5. Employee Issues and Retraining Possibilities

Employees may become concerned about the future viability of their work and the likelihood that they may be replaced by robots as a result of the development of AI. Companies need to address these concerns via open channels of communication, retraining initiatives, and the creation of brand-new employment roles that complement AI technology.

Artificial intelligence (AI) integration into company operations has the potential to bring about a number of advantages, including greater productivity, better decision-making, improved customer experiences, and more creativity. To be effective, firms must overcome challenges such data quality, privacy, ethics, a lack of skilled workers, system integration, legal restrictions, and employee concerns. Organizations may fully use AI and significantly enhance their operations and strategy by proactively tackling these challenges. Taking up the problems head-on makes this feasible.

Chapter Four

Automation

Artificial intelligence (AI), which stands for "artificial intelligence," and its connection to automation, a challenging and exciting issue, have received a lot of attention in recent years. Automation and artificial intelligence (AI) are two distinct but related ideas that have the potential to upend a number of industries and have a significant influence on how we live our daily lives. Let's start by delving further into the definitions of the phrases artificial intelligence (AI) and automation, and then evaluate how these two ideas affect and are impacted by one another, in order to explore this link.

The process of programming computers to do activities that ordinarily need the intellect of a human being is known as artificial intelligence (AI). These systems are designed to carry out operations including data analysis, pattern recognition, decision making, and experience-based learning, typically with the goal of progressively improving overall performance. The subfields of artificial intelligence (AI), which include computer vision, robotics, natural language processing, and machine learning, are just a few. It has uses in a broad range of industries, including manufacturing, finance, transportation, and healthcare.

Automation, on the other hand, is the use of technology to carry out tasks or processes with just a minimal level of human participation. This project aims to improve output while also streamlining procedures and improving efficiency. Automation may be used for everything from basic, repetitive tasks like data input or assembly line operations to more complex jobs like decision- and problem-solving. Data input and assembly line tasks are examples of the former. Businesses have found extensive use for it in the manufacturing, shipping, customer service, and information technology industries, to name just a few.

The relationship between AI and automation may take many different forms. Automation systems may be powered by artificial intelligence technologies since they will enable robots to see, understand, and respond to their immediate environment. By assessing items for faults, computer vision algorithms, for instance, might be used to automate quality control in manufacturing. To accomplish this, one would examine the items for defects. Natural language processing makes it feasible to automate customer support services via the use of algorithms that comprehend and respond to consumer inquiries. AI-powered chatbots are gaining popularity because they can provide quick help and replies while reducing the need for human interaction.

Additionally, automation is a crucial step in the creation and implementation of AI systems. Artificial intelligence systems typically need enormous volumes of data in order to learn and improve their effectiveness. Automation may be used to streamline the collection, processing, and labeling of these datasets, making them more accessible for use in the training of AI models. Automation may also automate the development and use of AI models, increasing the effectiveness and scalability of the whole process. The benefit of automation is this.

Automation and AI work together to deliver outcomes that are both useful and significant. On the one hand, combining automation with artificial intelligence offers the potential to increase output while lowering costs and improving accuracy. When routine and repetitive tasks are automated, businesses may reallocate their human resources to more challenging and creative tasks. By replacing workers in hazardous locations with robots or autonomous systems, automation powered by AI has the potential to improve safety.

However, there are a number of worries related to the relationship between AI and automation. One of the biggest sources of worry is the prospect of robots taking over human labor. There is a chance that certain job activities will become obsolete as automation technology advances, which could lead to societal injustices and unemployment. It's important to remember, however, that historically, the growth of automation has been accompanied with the introduction of whole new employment opportunities. This is because automation enables the emergence of whole new industries and economic sectors.

Another concern is the ethical issues that AI-driven automation raises. As artificial intelligence (AI) systems grow increasingly independent and capable of making decisions, fresh worries about bias, accountability, and openness have emerged. The need to ensure that AI algorithms are fair, impartial, and consistent with human values cannot be overstated. It is necessary to create ethical guidelines and legal regulations to regulate the use of automation and artificial intelligence. This will guarantee that the technology safeguards private data, maintains human agency, and lessens the possibility of unfavorable effects.

The relationship between automation and artificial intelligence is complex and dynamic. Artificial intelligence technologies, which give computers abilities akin to those of humans, enable automation. Automation also hastens the creation and use of AI systems. This link has the potential to transform whole sectors, boost productivity significantly, and improve the quality of life for everyone. However, technology also poses challenges in terms of job displacement and moral ramifications. In order to profit from both automation and artificial intelligence (AI), the proper balance between the two must be found while also addressing the issues they bring with them.

examining how AI is changing the labor economy and workforce

There is no doubting that AI is significantly changing the workforce and the job market. Artificial intelligence-based technologies are still being developed, and as a consequence, many tasks are being automated, human abilities are being improved, and even whole new job categories are being created. This change offers both possibilities and difficulties, which are both examined in more detail below.

• Automating Procedures That Were Previously Manual

Artificial intelligence (AI) is rapidly being used to automate routine and repetitive tasks that don't need human judgment or creativity. This includes duties including data entry, document processing, client support, and elementary analysis. This directly results in the loss of occupations that are focused on these activities, which has sparked worries about job relocation. However, it is important to remember that in the past, automation has led to the creation of employment in brand-new sectors. Additionally, there is a chance for individuals to move on to more challenging and gratifying jobs.

• Increasing the capabilities of people

By helping people in a range of vocations, artificial intelligence is also improving human capabilities. For instance, the capacity of AI-powered systems to sift through massive amounts of data and provide smart suggestions might help professionals make decisions more quickly and correctly. Workers may now focus on higher-level problem-solving, as well as innovation and creativity, as a result of this improvement. Artificial intelligence may help in fields like healthcare by recognizing illnesses, offering treatment options, and performing research, all of which can improve patient outcomes.

• The emergence of hitherto unrecognized job roles

New job categories that did not previously exist are being created as a consequence of the extensive use of AI. These careers usually include working with AI systems to accomplish certain objectives by making use of the tools such systems have to offer. For instance, both AI trainers and explainability specialists are required in the design, instruction, and interpretation of AI models. To ensure that AI technologies are utilized in a responsible and ethical way, data scientists and experts in AI ethics are in great demand. Additionally, as a result of artificial intelligence, there is a growing need for professionals in a number of industries, such as robotics, natural language processing, and machine learning.

• Skills needed and retraining

The talents that businesses are looking for in potential workers are changing as a result of the expanding use of AI. As more and more routine jobs are automated, there is a rising need for skills that complement artificial intelligence technologies. The importance of "soft skills" including critical thinking, creativity, problem-solving aptitude, and emotional intelligence is constantly increasing. The development of technical skills related to artificial intelligence (AI), such as data analysis, algorithm creation, and administration of AI systems, is also in demand. In order to provide employees with the necessary skills for today's dynamic labor market, programs aimed to reskill and upskill individuals are critically essential.

• The Effect on Specific Economic Sectors

AI is having a wide range of effects on several industries. For instance, manufacturing processes in the industrial sector are being drastically changed by robots and automation systems that are driven by artificial intelligence

(AI). Predictive analytics and autonomous vehicles are revolutionizing supply chain management and logistics in the transportation sector. AI is being used in the financial industry for algorithmic trading, fraud detection, and the provision of specialized financial services. AI is now being used in the healthcare sector for drug development, medical image analysis, and customized treatment. Workers will require industry-specific expertise and experience due to these advancements.

• Examining the Moral and Social Repercussions

Since AI has been used in the workplace, concerns have been raised about ethics and society. Artificial intelligence systems used in decision-making procedures like employment, lending, and criminal justice may introduce biases and prejudice into the system if they are not properly designed and controlled. Concerns have also been expressed about the security of personal data and information, as well as the possibility that social inequalities might be made worse by artificial intelligence. The creation of strict ethical frameworks, laws, and governance mechanisms is crucial to overcoming these obstacles and guaranteeing the ethical use of AI in the workplace.

Artificial intelligence (AI) is changing the workforce and the labor market by automating repetitive jobs, enhancing human ability, creating new job categories, and modifying skill requirements. There are concerns about job loss and moral considerations to take into account, but there is also room for innovation, higher productivity, and the emergence of new sectors. Proactive measures are needed to adapt to this transformation, such as reskilling programs, ethical standards, and laws that promote the egalitarian and inclusive use of artificial intelligence. If we acknowledge the promise of artificial intelligence (AI) and manage the challenges it offers, we will be able to manage the quickly evolving workplace and take use of AI technology for the good of society.

examining how AI could affect employment and the need for reskilling and upskilling

The potential impacts of AI on employment have sparked a lot of attention and debate. Artificial intelligence may automate a variety of tasks and job duties, but it also creates new possibilities and necessitates the need for retraining and additional education. Let's go further into the subject at hand to evaluate the effects and understand the importance of skill upgrading and retraining.

• A comparison of job losses and job creation

One of the numerous concerns about AI is the chance that it may destroy employment. The need for some jobs will decline as artificial intelligence (AI) technologies develop their ability to automate routine and repetitive activity. However, it is critical to remember the historical trend in which automation has resulted in the development of new job possibilities across a range of sectors. As AI automates more and more routine tasks, it frees up human employees to focus on more difficult tasks requiring critical thinking, problem-solving skills, and emotional intelligence. Making the most of AI systems' capabilities, managing their resources, and collaborating with them are more frequent professional duties.

• Modifying the Required Competency Level

The distribution of talents will change as a consequence of the use of AI in the workplace. Despite the fact that certain professional occupations may need less daily technical skills, the demand for talents that complement AI technology is anticipated to increase. "Soft skills" like critical thinking, creativity, and the capacity to solve complex issues, as well as emotional intelligence, are becoming more and more valued since they are difficult to automate. Additionally, technical skills related to AI, such as data analysis, machine learning, programming, and algorithm creation, are becoming more and more in demand. Worker upskilling and reskilling programs are unavoidably necessary to provide employees the skills they need to adjust to shifting demand.

• Programs for reskilling and upskilling

It is becoming more and more obvious that measures to retrain and upskill employees are required as AI continues to alter the labour sector. Reskilling is the process of learning entirely new skills for a different career, while upskilling is the process of enhancing current talents to match changing employment requirements. These programs come in a broad range of forms, such as online courses, career training, apprenticeships, and professional development initiatives. Governments, educational institutions, and other organizations must collaborate to design and implement effective training programs that provide people the skills they need to succeed in an artificial intelligence (AI)-driven employment market.

• Learning Is A Lifelong Process

The importance of ongoing education has received increasing emphasis as a result of the development of AI. Employees must continue their education to be marketable and versatile since technology advancements are always being produced. It is best to see the development of new talents and the enhancement of current ones as ongoing processes that take place throughout the course of a person's career rather than as singular events. The promotion of self-directed learning, the facilitation of accessible learning opportunities, and encouragement of a culture of continuous learning are crucial when it comes to preparing the workforce for the era of artificial intelligence (AI).

• Completing Skill Set Gaps

AI widens the already existing skills gap by increasing the demand for certain talents above the talent pool that is already accessible. Organizations and educational institutions must actively interact with one another and coordinate their efforts if this gap is to be closed. Industry collaborations, apprenticeship programs, and other types of work-integrated learning may help close the skills gap by offering hands-on training and modern education. Governments may take an active part in the creation of regulations and financial incentives that foster joint ventures between diverse businesses and academic institutions.

• Modifying the Process of Education

AI's impact on employment highlights the urgent need to update educational procedures in order to better educate students for professions of the future. Traditional educational approaches may not provide students with the skills and information needed to flourish in a world where artificial intelligence rules the roost. Early on in students' educational experiences, it is important to stress critical thinking, problem-solving, creative thinking, and digital literacy. Additionally, ideas and skills connected to AI should be included in the curriculum. Interdisciplinary learning and lifelong learning should also be encouraged. These need to be the top concerns in educational reform.

• New Situations and Roles in the Workforce

Even if AI has the potential to automate certain tasks, it will also provide new job possibilities. AI systems need to be developed, deployed, and maintained over time, all of which need specialized knowledge. Trainers of artificial intelligence, experts in explainability, data scientists, AI ethicists, and robotics engineers are some of the emerging job categories. Data scientists are among the other newest job categories. Working alongside AI systems, maximizing the capabilities provided by such systems, and ensuring the right and moral deployment of those capabilities are all necessary for these professions.

The potential effects of AI on employment are a complex and nuanced subject. AI has the potential to replace certain professions, but it will also provide new possibilities and need workers to retrain and pick up new skills. If we accept learning that lasts a lifetime, create programs that successfully upskill and reskill employees, bridge the gap in accessible skills, and modify our educational institutions, we can prepare the workforce for the changing labor market that is being driven by AI. In doing so, we will be able to use artificial intelligence technology to complement human abilities, encourage creativity, and develop a workforce that is more resilient and adaptable.

Chapter Five

Ethical Considerations

Artificial intelligence (AI) is the term used to describe the use of computer programming to simulate human intellect in order to carry out jobs that have traditionally been handled by people. AI has become increasingly pervasive in our daily lives, from personal gadgets and virtual assistants to sophisticated systems used in banking, healthcare, and transportation. While there are many opportunities and advantages that come with artificial intelligence, there are also some significant ethical concerns that need to be resolved before it can be used to its full potential. In this discussion, we will examine some of the most significant ethical issues raised by AI and consider possible solutions to those issues.

Fairness and bias both exist.

One of the most important moral issues that artificial intelligence raises is the potential for biased judgements. Massive volumes of data are used to teach AI systems, and if that material is biased or reflects societal preconceptions, the AI systems' operating algorithms may reinforce and magnify such prejudices. This may lead to unfair loan approvals, biased employment procedures, or racially biased police enforcement, among other discriminatory results.

It is crucial to make sure that AI systems are trained on datasets that are both varied and representative in order to discover a solution to this issue. One should consider the likelihood of biases while gathering data and attempt to minimize or eliminate them. Additionally, total openness is necessary for AI algorithms so that the decision-making process can be examined and audited. Implementing legislative frameworks that promote fairness and transparency in the use of AI may be able to allay some of these worries.

• Safety and discretion

Artificial intelligence usually relies on gathering and analyzing vast amounts of personal data. Due to the possibility of sensitive information being utilized improperly or accessed without consent, this poses privacy concerns. AI systems must be created with privacy considerations in mind and use strict security controls to prevent data breaches and unauthorized usage. Strict data governance mechanisms, such as encryption and anonymization techniques, may be implemented to protect people's privacy while still using AI effectively.

• Responsibility-taking and accountability are essential.

As artificial intelligence develops into a more self-sufficient entity, the issue of accountability and responsibility becomes more and more urgent. It is critical to determine who is responsible for any damage caused when AI systems make decisions or do actions with significant consequences. On the other hand, since AI systems may be challenging to comprehend and their decision-making processes could be cryptic, assigning accountability might be challenging.

Different legal frameworks and regulations must be developed in order to define accountability and duty in the use of artificial intelligence in order to handle this problem. Processes for auditing and elucidating how AI makes choices should be pushed, and the creators of AI systems and the organizations that use them should be held accountable for the actions and outcomes generated by such systems.

• Worker displacement and unfair economic opportunities

Because of how quickly AI technology is evolving, there are worries that job possibilities may disappear and that economic inequality would increase. The development of artificial intelligence and automation has the potential to result in the loss of a sizable number of employment. This is particularly true for industries that rely heavily on routine or repetitive tasks.

Society must prioritize reskilling and upskilling the working population in order to accommodate the changing nature of the labor market if it is to manage these challenges. Through the use of specialized education and training programs, people should be given the skills necessary to thrive in an economy driven by AI. In order to lessen the possible negative consequences that AI may have, governments and organizations should also look at future employment-related laws, such as universal basic income or job-sharing programs.

• Making moral decisions and ensuring they are consistent with your values

Artificial intelligence systems have the potential to independently make decisions that affect people's lives. It is crucial that these decisions be made in line with ethical principles and human values. Nevertheless, it is a challenging challenge that has to be taken on to figure out how to give AI systems the capacity to make moral judgments.

To guarantee that ethics are included into the core of AI system design, it is crucial for lawmakers, engineers, and ethicists to collaborate in an interdisciplinary manner. It is advised that ethical frameworks be included

149

into AI systems throughout creation, taking a broad range of cultural, social, and moral viewpoints into consideration. Additionally, via dialogue with the public and active engagement from the public, social norms and values that should guide the development and use of AI should be developed.

The ethical issues and issues that artificial intelligence raises must be addressed with a multifaceted approach. It requires proactive actions including the collection of diverse and representative data, the use of transparent algorithms, the provision of acceptable privacy safeguards, the existence of clear legislative frameworks, and the involvement of stakeholders. By taking these steps, we will be able to harness AI's revolutionary potential while also ensuring that it complies with our moral principles and values. As a consequence, we will be able to utilize AI responsibly and create a society that is more equal.

talking about things like openness, privacy, and prejudice in AI systems

In a wide range of industries, including social media, law enforcement, healthcare, and the financial sector, AI systems have become very popular and significant. However, the widespread use of AI brings up significant issues with bias, privacy, and system openness. We will examine these difficulties in detail throughout this discussion, as well as the effects they have on AI systems.

• Bias

In artificial intelligence (AI) systems, the concept of "bias" refers to the potential for discriminating results or unjust treatment that may occur from biases existing in the data that is used to train these systems. AI algorithms have the capacity to reinforce and amplify societal preconceptions, which might lead to unjust or discriminating outcomes. If the training data is not representative or varied, this risk rises. For instance, a biased AI algorithm in the hiring process may favor certain demographics or uphold gender or racial prejudices.

A number of significant actions must be made in order to eliminate bias in AI. The diversity, representativeness, and bias-freeness of the training data required to train AI models must be ensured at all costs. The first and most crucial step is this one. In order to provide a suitable representation of a range of demographics and prevent either underrepresentation or overrepresentation, this may be achieved by using diligent data collection approaches. To further the objective of broadening the variety of the training data, techniques like data augmentation and the creation of synthetic data may be used.

153

Another crucial element in the battle against discrimination is the openness of the AI algorithms that are being deployed. If the decision-making procedures used by artificial intelligence (AI) systems can be made transparent and understood, biases in such systems will be simpler to identify and eradicate. This may be done by using techniques like explainable AI, which makes the inner workings of AI algorithms understandable and allows them to be evaluated for bias.

• Privacy

In order to make informed decisions, artificial intelligence systems typically gather and analyze vast volumes of personal data. On the other hand, this poses a substantial challenge to maintaining people's privacy. Without authorization, illegal use, or poor handling of personal information may lead to significant privacy violations and rights violations.

When deploying AI systems, effective data governance mechanisms are necessary to preserve users' privacy. This involves the use of strong encryption and security measures to safeguard personal data at every stage of its lifetime, from collection to storage and analysis. It is also possible to protect people's identities while yet allowing for thorough analysis by using anonymization techniques.

The notion of "privacy by design" should act as a guiding principle while developing and deploying AI technologies. This entails incorporating privacy problems into system design from the outset, making sure that privacy protections are included into the system's architecture and functionality, and incorporating privacy considerations into system design from the outset. Legislative frameworks, such as data protection laws, also play a crucial role in setting standards for the protection of personal information and ensuring responsibility for data management practices.

• Transparency

The ability to understand and explain how artificial intelligence (AI) systems make decisions is referred to as "transparency" in this context. Transparent or "black box" AI algorithms provide challenges in terms of accountability, trust, and the ability to identify and remedy any biases or flaws they may include.

In order to establish trust and assure responsibility, transparency must be encouraged inside AI systems. Explainable AI techniques seek to crack open the "black box" of AI systems in order to get knowledge about how choices are made. The use of model interpretability approaches, such as the analysis of feature significance, the extraction of rules, or the creation of explanations for specific choices, may achieve this.

In addition to the technological precautions that have been implemented, regulatory actions may also play a significant role in ensuring transparency. By establishing rules that demand openness and auditing of AI systems, it may be able to prevent the adoption of AI algorithms that are nonsensical or unintelligible.

Additionally, the development of more transparent business processes may be aided by the building of an open culture inside organizations and the support of moral standards in the design and use of AI.

To properly address issues about bias, privacy, and transparency in AI systems, a multi-pronged approach is needed. It necessitates paying particular attention to the procedures used for data collection and representation, implementing strict privacy protection measures, fostering transparency via both technological and legal methods, and developing an ethical and responsible artificial intelligence ecosystem. If we solve these issues, we can develop artificial intelligence systems that are transparent, equitable, and considerate of users' privacy. This will guarantee that AI systems are used for both an individual's and society's overall advantage.

investigating the need for ethical AI development and governance systems

Artificial intelligence (AI) technology's rapid progress has created a wide range of new opportunities and the ability to totally transform a number of different sectors. However, it has also led to significant concerns over the ethical, social, and economic effects of the use of AI. It is urgently necessary to develop AI that is morally responsible and strong governance structures in order to allay these worries. We will look at the issues that made responsible AI development necessary as well as the need of governance structures throughout this discussion.

• Moral questions to think about

AI systems are able to make decisions on their own and have the potential to significantly affect people's lives in many different ways. Artificial intelligence must be operated in accordance with moral principles. Important ethical concepts include respect for one's right to privacy and other civil freedoms as well as fairness, responsibility, and transparency. Responsible AI development is necessary to make sure that these elements are taken into consideration throughout the design, development, and deployment of AI systems.

• Favoritism and discrimination

Artificial intelligence (AI) systems have the risk of accidentally amplifying and reinforcing preexisting biases seen in training data, which may have discriminatory effects. By making sure that training data is diverse and representative, including techniques for bias detection and mitigation, and promoting transparency in algorithmic decision-making processes, responsible AI development aims to eradicate prejudice. Principles and rules for enforcing fairness and preventing bias in artificial intelligence systems may be found in governance frameworks.

• It's crucial to have both transparency and trust.

When implementing AI, trust is a crucial element. A barrier to trust may be the users' and stakeholders' inability to comprehend and acquire important information about AI algorithms. The establishment of transparent AI systems, the development of understandable and interpretable algorithms, and the facilitation of auditing and inspection of decision-making processes are the three main pillars of responsible artificial intelligence development. In order to promote trust between users and AI providers and to guarantee transparency, governance frameworks have the power to create rules and laws.

• Privacy and Personal Information Protection

Artificial intelligence systems usually depend on the gathering and processing of enormous volumes of data, which raises concerns about the privacy and security of personal data. By adopting the ideas of privacy-by-design, implementing strong data security measures, and abiding with data protection laws, responsible AI development ensures that privacy is stressed from the very beginning. The process of defining guidelines for data processing practices, ensuring that informed consent is gained, and enforcing penalties for privacy breaches all depend heavily on governance structures.

- Accountability in addition to legal requirements

Questions of responsibility and guilt take on increased significance as AI systems grow more self-sufficient. The development of responsible artificial intelligence should include mechanisms for allocating blame and accountability for the deeds and choices of AI systems. To enable developers, organizations, and consumers to understand the boundaries and restrictions of AI systems, unambiguous guidelines must be provided to them. Governance frameworks may develop legal frameworks and rules to resolve culpability and accountability in circumstances where artificial intelligence (AI) systems do damage or make poor judgements.

• Economic and Social Impact

Technologies based on artificial intelligence (AI) have the potential to transform industries and labor markets, which might lead to job losses and rising economic inequality. Responsible AI development calls for consideration of the socioeconomic effects of AI deployment, investment in reskilling and upskilling initiatives, and investigation of legislation that addresses the potential negative effects of AI on employment. Developing policies and initiatives to lessen these harms and facilitate a fair transition to an economy driven by artificial intelligence (AI) might be made simpler by governance frameworks.

• Global initiatives for cooperation

Since the development of AI and its application are not constrained by national borders, they need international coordination and collaboration. Frameworks for the ethical development of artificial intelligence and for its governance should be created via international collaboration. Sharing best practices, coordinating ethical and legal obligations, and gathering data will all be made feasible as a result. International partnerships are able to promote AI development responsibly on a global scale and guarantee that AI is used for the benefit of mankind.

It is crucial to develop AI responsibly and to set up strong governance structures in order to solve the ethical, social, and economic issues that it raises. If we prioritize moral concerns, maintain transparency, safeguard privacy, encourage accountability, address socio-economic repercussions, and foster international collaboration, we will be able to harness the promise of AI while defending human values and interests. By making sure that AI is developed and governed responsibly, we can strive toward a future where it benefits every member of society.

Chapter Six

AI and Healthcare

The potentially revolutionary role that AI may play in the healthcare sector is now the subject of intense attention and research. Due to its ability to manage enormous volumes of data, identify trends, and make predictions, artificial intelligence has the potential to transform many areas of healthcare. The diagnosis and management of illnesses, individualized medicine, and administrative tasks are some of these aspects. All of these aspects might change as a result of AI. We will explore the transformative potential of AI in the healthcare sector during this discussion, as well as go more into a number of crucial areas where AI is significantly advancing the state of the art.

• The Condition's Diagnosis and Its Prognosis

In recent years, it has been clear that AI systems possess exceptional diagnostic and prognostic abilities. AI algorithms can identify patterns and provide precise projections by thoroughly analyzing vast amounts of medical data. Medical imaging, genetic data, and patient records are just a few examples of this data. For instance, AI models have shown to be quite accurate in spotting cancerous cells in radiological imaging, including lung scans and mammograms. These models have shown positive results in this regard. Early diagnosis and accurate prognosis have the potential to dramatically improve patient outcomes by enabling immediate interventions and tailored treatment plans.

• New Drug Development and Research

Finding novel medications and turning them into useful forms is a challenging, expensive, and time-consuming process. With the use of AI, this procedure may be streamlined and finished much more rapidly. Huge amounts of biological data, including genetic data, protein structures, and the outcomes of clinical trials, may be examined by algorithms that learn via machine experience in order to identify potential drug candidates and predict their efficacy. Artificial intelligence (AI)-powered systems may predict and optimize medication formulations, reducing the need for laboratory testing. By enabling faster and more accurate medication development, artificial intelligence may speed the delivery of innovative therapeutics to patients.

• Individualized medicine

AI has the ability to expand access to customized medicine by using patient-specific data to create personalised treatment regimens. A patient's genetic profile, medical history, and lifestyle characteristics may all be taken into consideration by AI algorithms to provide personalized therapeutic recommendations. By include patient-specific data in the algorithm, this is made possible. With this approach, the likelihood of any undesirable side effects might be minimized while the therapeutic benefits could be maximized. AI may also help forecast how patients will respond to certain medications, which can aid physicians in deciding on the best course of action and the right dose.

• The Use of Remote Monitoring and Telemedicine

The COVID-19 outbreak has sped up the use of telehealth and other remote monitoring technologies. A key aspect of AI's significance in many sectors is its capacity to provide remote patient monitoring, symptom tracking, and virtual consultations. Artificial intelligence-powered chatbots and other virtual assistants may gather patient data, provide basic medical advice, and prioritize patients based on their symptoms. With the use of AI algorithms, remote monitoring devices can evaluate patient data in real-time, such as vital signs and activity levels, and alert medical staff if anything seems out of the ordinary. This technology enhances patient comfort, eases the burden on healthcare providers' infrastructure, and makes it simpler for people to receive healthcare services.

• The efficiency of administrative practices

In the healthcare sector, artificial intelligence has the potential to automate a lot of administrative tasks, freeing up staff members to spend more time directly caring for patients. Medical record evaluation and information extraction using natural language processing (NLP) algorithms may streamline the process of describing and categorizing medical disorders. In the healthcare sector, AI-powered solutions may also assist with appointment scheduling, resource allocation optimization, and process management. By reducing the demands of administrative labor, AI has the potential to increase efficiency, reduce expenses, and enhance the entire experience of obtaining medical care.

There are still many challenges to be resolved despite the great promise for AI to improve healthcare. These include maintaining ethical standards, ensuring data privacy and security, removing biases from AI algorithms, integrating AI systems with the present healthcare infrastructure, and so on. The integration of AI technologies with the current healthcare infrastructure is another difficulty. In addition, it is important to remember that artificial intelligence should not be used in place of human knowledge in the healthcare industry, but rather as a tool to supplement it.

By facilitating personalized treatment, allowing remote monitoring and telemedicine, hastening drug development, enhancing administrative effectiveness, and enhancing sickness diagnosis and prognosis, AI has the potential to change healthcare. If we use the powers of artificial intelligence (AI), we can enhance patient outcomes, increase healthcare accessibility, and usher in a new age of precision medicine. However, careful deployment, legal frameworks, and ongoing research are crucial elements to fully realize the transformational promise of AI in healthcare while addressing the difficulties that are connected with it.

examining how AI is being used in drug development, customized medicine, diagnostics, and patient care

Let's examine each of these subjects in further detail now:

• Diagnostics

AI has already shown to have enormous promise for improving the accuracy of diagnosis across a range of medical disciplines. Machine learning algorithms are capable of accurately identifying patterns and diagnosing abnormalities in medical images such as X-rays, CT scans, and MRIs. For instance, AI has been used effectively to identify early signs of diabetic retinopathy in eye scans and to detect cancerous cells in mammograms. These two uses both entail imaging the eye. AI algorithms may also look at a patient's symptoms, medical history, and the outcomes of laboratory testing in order to help with illness diagnosis. If artificial intelligence is capable of generating rapid and accurate diagnoses, it has the potential to help medical professionals make better-informed treatment choices and eventually improve patient outcomes.

• Individualized medicine

The aim of customized medicine is to design treatment plans that are unique to each patient and take into consideration their unique characteristics. One of the most crucial tasks performed by AI in this field is the analysis of vast volumes of patient data, such as genetic profiles, medical records, lifestyle variables, and treatment results. In order to forecast how patients will respond to different therapies, machine learning algorithms may examine data to seek for patterns and connections. As a result, medical experts are able to choose the therapies that have the highest likelihood of being effective, identify the ideal dosage of medicine, and lower the danger of unfavorable side effects. In the realm of precision oncology, AI may help with the detection of specific genetic mutations in malignancies, the direction of targeted treatments, and the prediction of therapeutic response.

• Development of Novel Drugs

New drug discovery and development have historically been labor- and resource-intensive processes that often result in failure. These phases of the process might be totally changed by artificial intelligence. Machine learning algorithms may be used to identify potential drug candidates by analyzing vast amounts of biological data, including genetic information, protein structures, and chemical characteristics. Along with these skills, AI models can simulate and improve drug formulations, forecast drug-target interactions, and assess the likelihood that clinical trials will be successful. If artificial intelligence helps expedite the drug development process, it may help novel medications reach the market more rapidly and at a cheaper cost. Patients all throughout the globe will profit from this.

Care for patients

By allowing customized care planning, increasing medication adherence, and improving patient monitoring, the application of artificial intelligence (AI) is changing how patients are treated. A continuous surveillance of patients' vital signs, activity levels, and medication adherence is made possible by the use of remote monitoring devices that are coupled with artificial intelligence algorithms. This gives healthcare practitioners access to real-time information. Artificial intelligence (AI)-powered chatbots and virtual assistants may provide patients personalized medical advice, respond to their questions, and order patient cases based on their symptoms. AI may also help identify patients who are more likely to have issues or a readmission, allowing for proactive interventions and the delivery of tailored care.

AI may also be used to optimize patient flow, manage hospital workflow, and allocate resources. Utilizing predictive analytics models enables precise forecasting of patient intakes, optimal bed use, and efficient scheduling of procedural and surgical procedures. The identification of hospital-acquired infections, the detection of probable prescription mistakes, and the prediction of patient deterioration are other areas where predictive algorithms driven by AI may help. This allows early treatments and enhances patient safety.

It is critical to stress that a strong data infrastructure, privacy safeguards, and collaboration between medical professionals, data scientists, and regulatory organizations are necessary for the effective use of AI in these fields. It is crucial to consider ethical considerations including transparency, the elimination of bias, and accountability in order to guarantee the right implementation of AI in patient care.

The use of AI has considerably increased both the precision and timeliness of diagnosis. It makes customized therapy feasible by analyzing patient data and estimating treatment outcomes. By analyzing vast volumes of biological data, artificial intelligence might expedite the process of discovering novel medications. Artificial intelligence also improves patient care since it facilitates remote monitoring, encourages treatment compliance, and streamlines hospital procedures. It is vital to work together, follow existing laws, and make moral judgements if we are to fully profit from AI's advantages while simultaneously safeguarding patient safety and privacy.

highlighting the advantages and drawbacks of AI for the healthcare sector

- Increased Diagnosis and Accuracy Capabilities

To help in illness identification with a high degree of accuracy, AI algorithms have the potential to analyse enormous amounts of patient data, including medical images and clinical records. This may result in earlier diagnosis, more precise treatment plans, and ultimately improved patient outcomes.

• Individualized medicine

Individual patient data, including genetic profiles and medical histories, may be thoroughly analyzed using artificial intelligence in order to customize medicines and establish the most effective doses. With this approach, treatment effectiveness is increased while the danger of adverse effects is reduced and patient satisfaction is raised.

• Efficiencies and Spending Reductions

Artificial intelligence streamlines operations and automates administrative processes, all of which contribute to better resource allocation. As a consequence, operational efficiency improves, healthcare costs drop, and healthcare professionals are better able to focus on patient care.

• New Drug Development and Research

By analyzing vast volumes of biological data, forecasting how medications will interact with their targets, and refining drug formulations, artificial intelligence might hasten the drug development process. This might speed up the development of novel drugs and lower the price of learning via trial and error using more conventional approaches.

• Remote patient monitoring and telehealth services

The ability to remotely monitor patients, keep track of symptoms, and conduct virtual consultations is made feasible by AI-powered gadgets and virtual assistants. As a result, it is simpler for patients to get healthcare services, less demanding on healthcare organizations, and more practical for them.

• Executing research and data analysis

Huge datasets may be examined by AI algorithms in order to find patterns and correlations that may help researchers make significant discoveries and advance our knowledge of complex illnesses.

Objections to the Use of AI in Healthcare

• The accuracy and bias of the data

AI systems depend heavily on high-quality, diverse, and objective data when it comes to producing precise predictions. Biased artificial intelligence models and inaccurate outputs may be caused by data biases, insufficient or inconsistent data, a lack of representation, and these factors may even worsen already-existing healthcare imbalances.

• A lack of transparency and dialogue

Due to their complexity, AI models, especially in particular those built using deep learning methods, may be quite challenging to comprehend. Because AI systems lack transparency and explicability, it may be challenging for medical practitioners to trust them and understand their decision-making processes.

• Ethics-Related Issues

The use of AI in healthcare raises ethical issues related to patient privacy, informed consent, and the security of patient data. The protection of patient data and complete adherence to any relevant privacy regulations must be carefully considered when deploying AI.

• Legislative and regulatory challenges

The legal and regulatory frameworks that govern AI in the healthcare sector still have a lot of potential for expansion. To ensure a safe and responsible implementation of the technology, challenges including responsibility for AI-related failures, accountability, and regulatory clearance of AI-based medical devices are just a few examples of problems that need to be resolved.

• Interaction Between AI and Humans

It's crucial to keep in mind that artificial intelligence is meant to enhance and supplement qualified medical personnel rather than to replace them. In order to maintain patient-centered care and collaborative decision-making, it is essential to establish effective cooperation between AI systems and healthcare professionals.

• The capacity to both generalize and adapt

The ability of AI models to generalize their results and adjust to changing patient demographics, healthcare settings, or medical expertise may be challenging for those that have been trained on specialized datasets. If artificial intelligence models are to retain their accuracy and relevance over time, they must be constantly monitored, updated, and improved.

The use of AI in the medical industry has the potential to improve patient care, as well as provide better diagnosis, customized treatment, and cost savings. Limitations including inadequate data quality and transparency, as well as ethical questions and legal barriers, must be resolved in order to incorporate AI in the healthcare sector in a manner that is both responsible and successful. By first admitting the limits of the technology and then striving to reduce those limitations, the transformative potential of AI in the healthcare business may be harnessed.

Chapter Seven

Everyday Life

Artificial intelligence, commonly known as AI, is quickly taking on more significance in our daily lives and bringing about radical changes in a range of areas, including the manner in which we work, connect, enjoy ourselves, and even make decisions. From voice assistants like Siri and Alexa to recommendation systems on social networking sites and e-commerce websites, AI has almost permeated every part of our lives. We will explore the huge impact that AI has had on our daily lives throughout this discussion.

One of the most glaring instances of how artificial intelligence has altered our lives is the pervasive availability of intelligent gadgets and digital assistants. Artificial intelligence assistants that respond to voice commands, like Siri, Google Assistant, and Alexa, are becoming more prevalent in our homes. We may ask these helpers to do a number of things simply by speaking commands to them. These AI-powered personal assistants can answer questions, set reminders, play music, control smart home appliances, and even provide customized recommendations based on our preferences. We now engage with technology in a more natural and clear way as a result of the changes they have wrought.

Additionally, suggestions that we encounter on a number of online sites are personalized thanks to AI algorithms. Whether it be via the movie and TV program recommendations provided by Netflix, the custom playlists created by Spotify, or the buy recommendations provided by Amazon based on our browsing and shopping history, AI has significantly improved the quality of our digital experiences. Our past behaviors and preferences are taken into consideration when these recommendation algorithms sift through massive quantities of data to generate predictions and provide content that is relevant to our interests. As a result, learning about new categories of information and objects that we may not have previously encountered is now lot easy for us.

AI has significantly aided in the automation of time-consuming and repetitive processes at work. Human employees now have more time to focus on challenging and innovative tasks as a consequence. Several sectors, including manufacturing, transportation, and customer service, have adopted automation that is driven by AI in order to improve operations and increase efficiency. Robots and machines powered by artificial intelligence (AI), for example, are increasingly being used to do tasks like product assembly, quality control, and packaging. Companies utilize AI chatbots to handle client queries and provide prompt assistance to consumers. These advancements have increased productivity, but they also have the potential to open up new job opportunities that need the capacity to work productively with AI systems.

AI has also made significant strides in the healthcare sector, improving patient diagnosis, treatment, and overall care. Machine learning algorithms can examine a sizable amount of medical data, such as patient records, journal articles, and medical imaging. Based on the findings of this analysis, the algorithms may identify trends and make predictions. This helps medical practitioners identify illnesses more precisely and provide tailored treatment plans. Two examples of AI-powered medical devices that allow continuous monitoring of vital signs and early identification of possible health issues are wearable monitors and remote patient monitoring systems. AI-developed algorithms are also being used in clinical research, genomics, and drug development, all of which help to speed up the advancement of medicine.

On the other side, as AI's impact spreads, new concerns and challenges arise. One of the main concerns is the potential ethical fallout from AI decision-making. Accountability, transparency, and discrimination are issues that are becoming more and more of a worry as AI systems become more self-sufficient. Due to the fact that AI algorithms may only be as good as the data they are trained on, biased training material may cause the AI system to reinforce and magnify existing prejudices. The quality of AI algorithms depends on the data they are trained on. This has significant effects in many areas, including employment practices, the penal system, and loan judgements. It is a persistent issue that needs cautious consideration and regulation in order to achieve the objectives of reducing prejudice and guaranteeing justice in AI systems.

Another concern is how the development of AI may impact employment possibilities. Despite the fact that technology may boost productivity and provide new employment opportunities, there is worry that automation brought on by artificial intelligence (AI) may cause a significant loss of jobs. It's feasible that specific tasks and occupations that are easily mechanized might go out of style, forcing individuals to adapt their working methods and pick up new skills in order to stay employable. In order to provide people with the skills necessary to thrive in a future ruled by AI, it is crucial that governments and businesses engage in reskilling and upskilling efforts.

Security and privacy issues with artificial intelligence are additional worries. Massive amounts of personally identifiable information are collected and processed by AI systems, which raises the possibility of data breaches and unauthorized access. Making ensuring that user data is secure and that sufficient security measures are put in place is crucial to maintaining trust and safeguarding individual privacy.

human daily lives have been significantly impacted by artificial intelligence, which has invaded many aspects of human life. It has improved healthcare, changed workplace productivity and efficiency, and produced customized experiences in entertainment and online services. It has also improved the usability and accessibility of technology. To maximize the potential of AI while also ensuring that its benefits will be evenly dispersed, it is crucial to address ethical issues, create plans for the likelihood that employment may be disrupted, and prioritise privacy and security.

discussing smart homes, AI-powered virtual assistants, and customized suggestions

The increasing use of AI-powered virtual assistants, smart homes, and tailored recommendations in our daily lives is changing the way we engage with technology, manage our homes, and consume media. We will go further into these topics and look at how they affect our daily experiences and activities throughout this discussion.

Many households now have virtual assistants like Siri, Google Assistant, and Alexa. For their users, these assistants carry out a range of duties. These voice-activated assistants supported by AI provide us a straightforward, hands-free way to interact with our devices and do a range of activities, enabling us to accomplish more. Our interactions with technology have been made simpler by virtual assistants in a number of ways, including the capacity to set reminders, respond to questions, play music, manage smart home devices, and even purchase groceries.

We can now manage and control our living areas in ways that were not before feasible because to the development of artificial intelligence (AI) and the Internet of Things (IoT). Numerous AI-powered gadgets, such as smart appliances, lighting controls, security cameras, and thermostats, may be integrated into a single smart home ecosystem. It is simple to integrate in this way. We can automate and remote-control a number of components of our houses thanks to this connectedness. With only our smartphones or by giving commands to virtual assistants, we could, for instance, adjust the temperature, switch on or off the lights, monitor the activities of security cameras, and even turn on the appliances in our houses. When our homes are automated and controlled to this degree, convenience, energy efficiency, and safety all enhance.

Giving consumers customised recommendations made by AI algorithms is currently standard practice on a broad range of internet sites. The development of customized recommendations across a number of platforms, including streaming services like Netflix and Spotify and e-commerce websites like Amazon, has profoundly changed how we discover new material and engage with it. In order to provide suggestions that are specifically tailored to each individual user and that are in accordance with their interests, AI algorithms analyse enormous quantities of data, including our browsing history, purchase behavior, and user preferences. These algorithms learn new information over time and adjust their behavior, continuously refining their suggestions to provide consumers a more unique and engaging experience. We can now much more easily locate new films, television shows, music, books, and other products that are catered to our own tastes as a result.

Smart homes powered by AI, virtual assistants, and tailored recommendations have an impact that goes far beyond practicality and entertainment. These technologies have the power to boost our overall well-being, increase our productivity, and free up more of our time. By giving us more time to focus on more important tasks, virtual assistants increase both our productivity and our capacity to strike a good balance between work and life. For instance, we may utilize smart thermostats that learn our preferences and automatically regulate the temperature instead of manually setting the thermostat to achieve greater comfort and lower energy use.

Additionally, personalized suggestions result in a more immersive and captivating online experience. By exposing us to unusual and different options that we would not have otherwise encountered, AI algorithms might extend our perspectives. They do this by making recommendations for content and goods that are especially catered to our unique interests. Because it helps businesses to provide more individualized customer experiences, which in turn increases customer pleasure and loyalty, this has a big influence on many different industries, including the entertainment, media, and e-commerce sectors.

The employment of AI with the technologies that are now accessible is not without its challenges and worries, however. Privacy and data security issues are crucial, especially when it comes to virtual assistants and other smart home devices that collect and handle personal data. By carefully managing user information and making sure that efficient security measures are always in place, it is essential to maintain confidence and safeguard individual privacy.

Making personalized recommendations also has the issue of algorithmic bias and lack of transparency. Biases that are already present in the data itself might be perpetuated by AI algorithms' strong dependence on past data. For instance, biased streaming service suggestions or biased search results may help to maintain existing social prejudices and limit one's exposure to other viewpoints. To lessen the effects of these issues, it is crucial to promote justice, accountability, and openness in the development and use of AI algorithms.

Artificial intelligence-powered virtual assistants, smart homes, and tailored suggestions are becoming features of everyday life. They have totally changed how we interact with technology, manage our homes, and hunt for new knowledge and products. Numerous advantages are provided by these technologies, such as comfort, productivity, and customized experiences. Nevertheless, in order to ensure that AI-powered systems will continue to enhance our lives while abiding by ethical norms, it is imperative to address issues about privacy, security, and algorithmic bias.

Examining anticipated advancements in consumer AI technology in the future

Consumer AI technology has made significant advancements over the last several years, and it is thrilling to think about the future innovations that might have a big impact. In this discussion, we will explore some possible consumer AI technology advancements that may be on the horizon as well as the potential impact these advancements may have on our daily lives.

- Significantly enhanced Natural Language Processing (NLP)

In the near future, significant progress is expected to be made in the processing of natural language, which allows AI systems to understand and react to human language. Future advancements could make it possible for speech recognition to be more precise, contextual understanding to be more advanced, and language creativity to be more advanced. This may lead to more fluid and natural interactions with AI-powered gadgets

212

and virtual assistants, which would make communication more intuitive and natural.

An AI that is aware of its environment

Consumer AI is expected to become more context-aware in the near future, meaning that it will evaluate a larger variety of factors, such as the user's location, the time of day, past interactions, and personal preferences. AI would be able to provide advice, assistance, and services that are even more specifically customized and appropriate since it has this contextual awareness. For instance, a system powered by artificial intelligence may suggest nearby restaurants to a user based on the user's present location and favored cuisine.

- AI with emotions

Emotional AI, also known as affective computing, focuses on recognizing and responding correctly to human emotions. Future consumer AI systems could be equipped with emotional intelligence, enabling items to recognize and react to the emotions of their consumers. This may lead to interactions that are more personalized and compassionate, with AI systems adapting their responses in response to the user's emotional state. A virtual assistant may, for instance, provide consoling words or advice when it detects that a user is feeling unfavorable emotions like stress or despair.

• Improvements in Computer Vision

Computer vision, a branch of artificial intelligence that equips machines with the capacity to interpret and understand visual input, is poised to make significant technical strides. Consumer AI devices may have better image recognition abilities in the not too distant future. Based on images and videos, these gadgets will be able to identify objects, people, and even emotions. This has the potential to be used in a number of settings, such as enhanced security systems, augmented reality experiences, and photo search capabilities.

• combining the Internet of Things (IoT) with artificial intelligence.

It is projected that the Internet of Things and AI will integrate more quickly, creating a more intelligent and linked environment. Devices with AI capabilities will be able to gather and process data from a range of sensors and Internet of Things gadgets. As a result, these gadgets will be able to provide services that are more contextually and personally relevant. As an example, a smart home system driven by artificial intelligence (AI) may lower total energy usage by doing data analysis on information obtained from smart thermostats, lighting systems, and occupancy sensors.

- Individual AI assistants

It's feasible that personal AI assistants may develop into creatures that are even more capable and proactive in the future. These assistants are capable of managing a greater range of duties on their own, such as appointment scheduling, money administration, and providing support with challenging decision-making. By using machine learning and predictive analytics, these assistants would become more capable of detecting the desires and preferences of users, anticipating their needs, and providing guidance and support that are appropriate for the user's particular scenario.

• Transparent and moral artificial intelligence

As the usage of AI technology spreads, it will become more and more important to have AI systems that are transparent and ethical. Future AI development for consumer usage should prioritize justice, accountability, and openness. Efforts must be taken to eliminate biases, protect user privacy, and ensure that end users can understand and communicate with AI systems. This will guarantee that AI technology is advantageous to society as a whole and boost people's faith in it.

These prospective developments in consumer artificial intelligence technology have the power to significantly alter our everyday lives and routines. They have the potential to lead to more customized and natural interactions with technology, allowing AI systems to seamlessly integrate themselves into many aspects of our everyday lives. The need to ensure that artificial intelligence technology continues to function as a tool that allows and develops human skills, as well as the ethical consequences of these advancements, must all be carefully considered.

Chapter Eight

Data Privacy

A thorough investigation is necessary of the intricate and diverse interaction between AI and data privacy. On the one hand, artificial intelligence technologies have the potential to significantly enhance civilization by allowing improvements in a number of industries, including healthcare, transportation, and education. However, the broad use of AI raises questions regarding the security and privacy of personal information.

Data is a critical component of AI systems' training and decision-making processes. To attain high levels of accuracy and performance, they often need substantial volumes of varied and representative data. Personal information such as names, addresses, medical histories, financial information, and even behavioral patterns may be found in this data. As people may not be aware of how their data is being used or who has access to it, privacy problems may arise from the gathering and use of such data by AI systems.

The risk of data leaks is one of the key privacy issues raised by AI. Insufficient security may make AI systems appealing targets for hackers attempting to steal the private data they contain. Unauthorized access, use, or disclosure of personal data may result in identity theft, financial fraud, or other types of damage to people. This is known as a data breach.

Furthermore, AI systems have the capacity to examine and draw conclusions about sensitive data even from apparently unimportant data bits. AI can find patterns, correlations, and links in data that may not be obvious to humans by using machine learning algorithms. Due to the fact that personal characteristics, interests, and behaviors of people may be derived from apparently unrelated data, this raises worries about the possibility of inadvertent privacy breaches.

The possibility for algorithmic bias in AI systems, which may have privacy consequences, is another difficulty. AI algorithms may reinforce and magnify preexisting prejudices if they are trained on biased or discriminating data, which can result in unfair or discriminatory outputs. For instance, if the training data is skewed towards particular features, an AI system employed in recruiting procedures may unintentionally prejudice against certain demographic groups.

Several actions may be made in the context of AI to solve these issues and safeguard data privacy. First and foremost, while developing AI systems, businesses and developers should put privacy first. This entails integrating privacy issues into an AI system's design from the beginning and during its entire existence. Organizations may reduce the risks related to data privacy by putting in place privacy-enhancing measures such data anonymization, encryption, and access restrictions.

Accountability and transparency are also essential. Organizations should be open and honest about how they gather data, explain to people why it will be used, and provide them genuine control and choices over their data. Furthermore, procedures for getting informed permission should be in place, ensuring that people are aware of and consent to the collection and use of their data for AI purposes.

In the context of AI, regulation and law are essential for preserving data privacy. Governments and regulatory organizations should create and implement strict privacy regulations that handle the particular difficulties presented by AI. These regulations should lay out precise rules for data use, permission, accountability, and openness. Additionally, legal frameworks have to support the adoption of privacy-preserving technology and provide incentives for ethical AI creation and use.

In a future driven by AI, maintaining data privacy requires a strong commitment to education and awareness. People need to be aware of the possible advantages and threats of

AI, as well as their alternatives and rights with regard to data privacy. The general public and experts in AI-related professions, such as data science and computer engineering, should both be made aware of privacy best practices and ethical implications.

It is important to pay close attention to the complicated and developing interaction between artificial intelligence and data privacy. While AI has enormous potential to enhance society, it also presents problems for data privacy. We may work toward a balance that leverages the advantages of AI while preserving people's right to privacy by embracing privacy-by-design principles, encouraging openness and accountability, establishing suitable rules, and encouraging education and awareness.

examining the gathering, holding, and use of personal data in AI systems

The gathering, storing, and use of personal data in AI systems is a crucial issue that requires careful thought and ethical behavior. To guarantee privacy, security, and ethical usage as AI technologies continue to advance and penetrate many facets of our life, it is critical to look at how personal data is managed.

The gathering of personal information is a prerequisite for developing and using AI systems. Large and varied datasets are often used by AI systems to identify patterns and arrive at reliable predictions or judgments. This information may include many kinds of personal data, such as names, addresses, contact information, financial and health records, surfing patterns, and social media activity. It is essential to collect this information legally, openly, and with the informed agreement of the people in question.

AI systems should put a high priority on security and protection against unwanted access when storing personal data. To stop data breaches and protect confidentiality, strong data security measures including encryption, access limits, and safe storage procedures should be put in place. To lessen the danger of exposure, organizations must also think about data reduction techniques, retaining just the relevant and essential data needed for AI operations.

Furthermore, privacy rules and regulatory regulations should be followed while using personal data in AI systems. Organizations should be careful to specify the goals for which personal data is acquired and should outline those goals in detail. There should be consent systems in place that allow people to provide their informed permission for the use of their data. Data processing must also respect individual rights, including the right to access, correct, and remove personal information.

The possibility of algorithmic bias must be taken into account when employing personal data in artificial intelligence systems. When labeling the training data, bias might be unintentionally introduced during the data collection and preparation steps or via biased human judgment. Biased data has the potential to reinforce current social imbalances and produce biased results. To reduce bias and make sure fair and equitable AI systems, it is essential to carefully choose and diversity training data.

Organizations should place a high value on accountability and openness to encourage the ethical use of personal data in AI. Individuals should be informed about the data acquired, the goals for which it will be used, and the rights they possess by means of clear and succinct privacy rules. In order for people to understand how AI systems use personal data to generate judgments or predictions, organizations should be open about the underlying procedures. Additionally, accountability frameworks like audits and compliance frameworks may support ensuring compliance with ethical and privacy norms.

Regulations are essential for controlling how personal data is gathered, stored, and used by AI systems. In order to ensure that people's privacy rights are safeguarded, governments and regulatory organizations should adopt comprehensive privacy rules that meet the particular difficulties presented by AI. Clear norms for data processing, permission requirements, openness, and accountability should be included in these legislation. Data protection and ethical AI techniques are supported by adherence to privacy laws, such as the General Data Protection Regulation (GDPR) in the European Union.

Initiatives to raise awareness and educate the public are crucial if we want to enable people to make informed choices about their personal data. People must be aware of the repercussions of sharing their data as well as the advantages and disadvantages of using AI systems. To encourage a more privacy-conscious culture, educational programs should prioritize fostering digital literacy, privacy literacy, and data protection practices.

Personal data gathering, storage, and use in AI systems need careful consideration and ethical behavior. Throughout the whole lifetime of AI systems, organizations must give top priority to privacy, security, transparency, and responsibility. We can achieve a balance that utilizes the potential of AI while preserving individual privacy rights by adhering to legal requirements, implementing privacy-enhancing technology, minimizing algorithmic bias, and encouraging education and awareness.

Investigating the issues and possible solutions for privacy protection in the era of AI

Due to the growing gathering, analysis, and use of personal data, protecting privacy presents a number of issues in the age of AI. Among these difficulties are the enormous volumes of data being produced, the possibility of re-identification, algorithmic bias, and the need to strike a balance between privacy and innovation. The AI age offers a number of opportunities to overcome these issues and protect privacy, however.

• Data reduction

Data minimization is one of the main privacy protection tenets. Organizations should only acquire, store, and retain personal data that is required for the specific goal. Reduced data collection lowers the danger of illegal access and subsequent damage. Further privacy protection may be provided by anonymization methods including deleting or encrypting personally identifying information.

Security by Design

AI systems should include privacy issues from the beginning. According to Privacy by Design principles, AI system design and development should include privacy controls and protections. The use of privacy-enhancing technology, privacy impact analyses, and privacy-conscious behavior are all examples of this. The hazards related to personal data may be reduced by proactively addressing privacy.

• Strict Security Procedures

To secure personal data in AI systems, robust security measures are essential. Both data in transit and at rest should be protected by encryption. To prevent illegal access, access restrictions, multi-factor authentication, and secure storage techniques should be used. Regular security audits and vulnerability analyses aid in identifying and addressing possible system flaws.

• Consent and openness

Prior to collecting and utilizing someone's personal information, you must have that person's informed permission. Information on the reasons for data collection, the kinds of data being collected, and how it will be used should be provided by organizations in a clear and intelligible manner. Building trust with people and empowering them to take control of their data requires transparency.

• Automated Fairness and the reduction of bias

Fairness and bias reduction must be taken into consideration while creating and training AI systems. Inconsistent results from biased training data might reinforce social prejudices. Therefore, it is important to properly select data sets to guarantee inclusiveness and representativeness. AI systems may be monitored and audited often to assist identify and reduce bias. Additionally, interpretability approaches may be used to comprehend and justify the judgments made by AI systems, assuring justice and accountability.

• Privacy Rules and Regulations

In the era of AI, governments and regulatory organizations are essential for preserving privacy. The GDPR and related frameworks, which provide comprehensive privacy standards, set out legal duties for corporations around data protection, individual rights, and responsibility. Organizations are encouraged to value privacy via effective enforcement measures and penalties for non-compliance.

Government organizations may also create specialized groups or projects to supervise the regulation of AI and privacy, offering guidelines and criteria for ethical AI research.

• User Education and Empowerment

It is essential to inform people about their privacy rights, the dangers posed by AI systems, and privacy-enhancing procedures. Programs that promote privacy literacy may assist people in understanding the ramifications of sharing their data, empowering them to make wise decisions. To enable people to manage their privacy choices, user-centric tools such as privacy settings, access restrictions, and intuitive interfaces should be made available.

• Responsible AI and ethical issues

The development and use of ethical AI should be seen in the larger perspective of privacy protection. Organizations need to abide by moral principles that support responsibility, openness, justice, and society welfare. Responsible AI techniques, such as carrying out ethical impact analyses and taking into account many viewpoints, may assist in identifying and reducing possible privacy problems.

In the era of AI, privacy protection demands a thorough and multifaceted strategy. We can overcome the difficulties and protect privacy in the AI era while fostering innovation and societal benefits by implementing data minimization practices, incorporating privacy by design, ensuring strong security measures, obtaining informed consent, addressing algorithmic bias, complying with privacy regulations, promoting user empowerment and education, and embracing responsible AI practices.

Chapter Nine

AI and Work Landscape

The development of artificial intelligence (AI) has significantly altered the nature of employment, causing revolutionary shifts in a wide range of professions and sectors. In addition to automating monotonous and normal operations, AI technologies like machine learning, natural language processing, and robotics have made it possible to create sophisticated systems that are capable of making complicated decisions and solving problems. This has given people and organizations both opportunity and problems.

The automation of tedious and boring labor is one of the major implications of AI breakthroughs on the workplace. AI-powered solutions are progressively replacing manual labor and routine data processing in these positions. since a result of this automation, efficiency and productivity have grown since AI can work nonstop without getting tired and perform jobs more quickly. It has, however, also sparked worries about the displacement of employees in these industries, since they could have to move into other professions that call for more sophisticated skills and knowledge.

Furthermore, AI has made outstanding strides in fields like computer vision and natural language processing. As a consequence, chatbots, virtual assistants, and other AI-powered communication tools have become popular. By giving prompt and precise answers to queries, these technologies have improved user experiences and simplified customer service processes. In certain situations, firms have been able to do without human customer service employees as a consequence. While this change has increased productivity and decreased costs, it has also brought attention to the significance of learning new skills that supplement AI, such as emotional intelligence and decision-making capabilities.

Knowledge-based occupations have been significantly impacted by AI developments as well. For instance, AI-powered software can evaluate voluminous legal precedents and documents, facilitating quicker and more precise legal research in the subject of law. Similar to this, AI may support medical diagnosis by reviewing patient data and recommending possible treatments based on trends and patterns. While these technologies improve professionals' skills, they also raise concerns about the moral ramifications of relying on AI to make important decisions and the possibility for bias in AI systems.

The area of industrial automation has also undergone a revolution because to the incorporation of AI in manufacturing and robots. Cobots (collaborative robots) and intelligent robots may carry out difficult activities in the manufacturing, logistics, and other sectors of the economy. These robots can adapt to new jobs using machine learning techniques, thus they are not just useful for monotonous assembly line work. While improved productivity and accuracy may result from this automation, there are also worries regarding the effect on employment levels and the need to reskill personnel to work with or manage these robotic systems.

As AI technologies advance, new employment possibilities are opening up. Data science, machine learning, and AI ethics knowledge are needed for the creation and upkeep of AI systems. These specialist experts are in greater demand, which has led to the creation of new employment categories and career routes. In addition, the need for human control and regulation of AI systems has given rise to positions like explainability experts and AI ethicists, who guarantee accountability, transparency, and justice in AI decision-making procedures.

The nature of labor has undergone a fundamental transformation as a result of AI breakthroughs. Despite the fact that automation and AI-powered systems have improved production and efficiency, they have also created issues with job displacement and the need for reskilling. The use of AI in a variety of sectors calls for the creation of fresh knowledge and abilities as well as an analysis of the moral ramifications and biases ingrained in AI algorithms. People, companies, and politicians must adapt to and embrace AI technology as the workplace environment changes, taking into account the social and economic ramifications of these developments.

examining anticipated changes in the labor market and the need for retraining

The work market will be significantly impacted by the quick improvements in technology, notably in the areas of automation and artificial intelligence (AI). AI has the ability to restructure sectors, generate new employment opportunities, and alter the skills necessary for different professions as it continues to develop. The workforce must be proactive in becoming retrained and upgraded in order to keep up with the shifting needs of the labor market as a result of this transition.

The automation of repetitive and ordinary jobs is one of the main implications of AI and automation on the labor market. Manual labor-intensive jobs and activities that are amenable to codification and automation run the danger of being replaced by AI-driven systems. For instance, in the industrial industry, robots may replace human workers in jobs like assembly line labor. Although this automation boosts productivity and efficiency, it may also force people in these professions to move into other tasks requiring more advanced skills, such programming, maintenance, or supervisory duties.

It's crucial to remember that, even if automation may destroy certain employment responsibilities, it also opens up new possibilities. Specialized knowledge is needed for the creation and upkeep of AI systems as well as the need for human monitoring and control. New positions in fields including data science, machine learning, AI ethics, and explainability become available as a result. Additionally, there is a rising need for individuals who can collaborate with AI systems and take use of their capabilities to improve productivity and decision-making as AI technologies infiltrate many sectors.

The shifting skill needs within current occupations are another component of the employment market transition brought about by AI. Workers in practically every industry will need to develop new skills to stay relevant as AI automates basic activities. For instance, employees in the customer service industry, where chatbots and virtual assistants are becoming more prevalent, will need to have AI-complementing skills like empathy, critical thinking, and problem-solving ability. Similar to how professionals in knowledge-based fields like law and healthcare will need to adjust to AI-powered technologies that can help with research and diagnosis, forcing them to concentrate on higher-level analysis and decision-making, are also required in these fields.

Retraining and upgrading skills are required across all businesses and professions. It is a prerequisite that affects employees at all levels of the labor market. In order to be competitive, employees must constantly refresh their skill sets as technology develops at a fast rate. Individuals must be proactive in detecting growing skill needs and gaining the requisite information via training programs, certifications, online courses, and other educational resources. Lifelong learning has become vital.

Reskilling the workforce is a team effort rather than the solo duty of an individual. Governments, educational institutions, and employers all play a significant part in easing the transition. Employers must make investments in training initiatives and provide workers the chance to advance their skills. Institutions of higher learning must modify their courses to include topics linked to AI and encourage interdisciplinary thinking. To promote a seamless transition and address any disparities resulting from employment market adjustments, governments should assist reskilling projects via financing, incentives, and partnership with industry players.

It is important to remember that reskilling is a continuous process rather than a one-time occurrence. As technology develops, so will the labor market's need for expertise. As a result, developing a culture of continuous learning is essential for people and organizations to prosper in the workplace of the future.

AI and automation may cause labor market disruptions, thus it's important to proactively reskill and upskill the workforce. While automation may displace certain work responsibilities, it also opens up new career prospects in developing industries. Workers in all sectors need to concentrate on higher-level jobs that call for human judgment and creativity while learning new skills that complement AI. To achieve a seamless transition and address any disparities, reskilling initiatives should entail cooperation between people, employers, educational institutions, and governments. Individuals and organizations may navigate the changing employment market and take advantage of the possibilities given by AI developments by adopting lifelong learning and adaptation.

Investigating the potential for human-AI cooperation and new employment prospects

The potential for human-AI cooperation has the power to completely alter the employment market and open up new options for employees. Although there are worries that artificial intelligence (AI) will replace human employees, the truth is that AI technologies operate best when integrated with human talents, fostering synergistic teamwork that may promote creativity, productivity, and problem-solving.

Knowledge-intensive professions are one area where human-AI cooperation is already making substantial progress. Professionals may use AI-powered technologies to help with jobs that call for data analysis, research, and decision-making. For instance, in the healthcare industry, clinicians give the crucial human judgment and knowledge while AI algorithms scan medical data and diagnostic pictures to help in diagnosis. The delivery of healthcare is made more precise and effective because to this teamwork. Similar to this, AI-powered software can sort through enormous volumes of data in the legal and financial sectors and provide insights, freeing experts to concentrate on intricate legal strategy or investment choices.

Collaboration between humans and AI may also foster innovation and creativity. Large data sets may be used by AI systems to produce ideas, trends, and recommendations that help people explore new options and reach wise judgments. Designers use their aesthetic sensibility and contextual awareness to develop creative solutions while AI technologies may aid produce a variety of design possibilities. By enhancing human potential and broadening the range of possibilities, human-AI cooperation fosters innovation.

Customer service and engagement is another sector that is seeing the emergence of human-AI cooperation. Artificial intelligence (AI)-powered chatbots and virtual assistants can answer common client questions, freeing up human customer care representatives to tackle more complicated or specialized problems. This partnership guarantees effective and customized client experiences while lightening the strain on human employees. Voice assistants like Amazon Alexa or Google Assistant, where users interact with AI-powered systems for things like setting reminders or receiving information, are another example of how humans and AI may work together to perform everyday chores.

New employment possibilities that require collaborating with AI systems are emerging as a result of the integration of AI technology in sectors like manufacturing and logistics. There is a need for employees who can run, maintain, and program these robotic and automated systems as they proliferate. Cobots, or collaborative robots, are designed to work alongside people to increase productivity and safety. Employing their own judgment, flexibility, and problem-solving skills, workers might assume supervisory responsibilities, controlling and supervising the operation of AI-powered systems.

Furthermore, a variety of specialist talents are needed for the creation and implementation of AI systems. Jobs in data science, machine learning, and AI ethics are becoming more and more available. Researchers and engineers in AI are needed to create algorithms and models, while data scientists are required to gather and evaluate data. AI ethics need the use of experts who can guarantee justice, accountability, and transparency in AI systems. Communication and interaction abilities between humans and AI are necessary for explaining AI judgments to users and fostering their confidence. These newly developing positions underline the need for cross-disciplinary knowledge and AI-human cooperation.

Addressing issues like bias in AI algorithms, ethical concerns, and the effect on employment displacement is crucial if human-AI cooperation is to realize its full potential. To create AI systems that reflect human values, reduce biases, and preserve human supervision, collaboration between AI engineers and domain experts is essential. To foster a symbiotic connection between humans and AI, reskilling programs and educational efforts should be developed to provide people the skills necessary to work successfully with AI technology.

Collaboration between humans and AI has a wide range of potential applications. AI technology integration has the potential to improve human talents, stimulate creativity, and provide new career possibilities. We can increase levels of productivity, efficiency, and creativity by fusing the capabilities of people with AI systems. It is crucial to promote multidisciplinary cooperation, address ethical issues, and provide people the training and knowledge they need in order to adapt to and succeed in this changing labor market in order to fully achieve the promise of human-AI collaboration.

Conclusion

As we conclude "ARTIFICIAL INTELLIGENCE 2023," we find ourselves at a turning point, on the cusp of an era poised for profound change. The journey thus far has illuminated how to leverage artificial intelligence (AI) for personal and professional gain, unveiling its tremendous potential along the way. Now equipped with knowledge and perspective, it is time to reflect on our discoveries and prepare for the exciting future ahead.

Throughout this book, we have explored the many facets of AI, beginning with its origins and foundational concepts, and progressing to its applications across various business sectors. We have seen how AI is streamlining operations through automation and predictive analytics, enhancing customer experiences via intelligent virtual agents and personalized recommendations, and revolutionizing healthcare by enabling precise diagnostics and tailored treatments.

We have also delved into the ethical implications of AI, acknowledging the responsibility that comes with such power. Fairness, transparency, and accountability must be top priorities for artificial intelligence to continue rapid development. This will ensure AI's benefits are distributed equitably and any potential risks are mitigated.

AI has come a long way, but still has far to go before realizing its full potential. The evolution of artificial intelligence will be an endless process, continually pushing the boundaries of innovation and unlocking new possibilities. As technology accelerates, we will face increasing challenges and opportunities that will test our ability to stay engaged and adaptable.

Maintaining a flexible, proactive mindset is essential to capitalize on AI's market entrance. As the technology rapidly advances, we must embrace lifelong learning to keep our skills and knowledge current. Combining human ingenuity with AI's analytical power can yield groundbreaking results, so seeking collaborative opportunities is key. Stay abreast of the latest developments and trends in your industry, and leverage this insight to give yourself an edge over competitors.

Remember, AI's real strength is not replacing human jobs, but augmenting human capabilities and potential. By embracing artificial intelligence as an empowering tool, we can reimagine how we work, think, and create. Let us welcome AI to enhance our productivity, open new frontiers for creativity, and solve the world's greatest challenges.

In summary, "ARTIFICIAL INTELLIGENCE 2023" has equipped you with the knowledge, insights, and strategies to successfully navigate the AI landscape and harness opportunities for transformation. The journey has only just begun, and the choices we make today will profoundly impact the future we build. Embrace artificial intelligence, adapt to its rapid changes, and let it drive us toward a future defined by innovation, progress, and human-centered values.

Tapping into one of the decade's most significant trends and seizing AI's market entrance is a task for the present moment. Let us embark on this incredible adventure together, sculpting a world where AI and human intellect synergize to create a future beyond imagination. The age of artificial intelligence has arrived, and with the right knowledge and effort, the possibilities are virtually endless.